Parent's Quick Start Guide to Dyslexia

Parent's Quick Start Guide to Dyslexia provides parents and caregivers with an immediate overview of dyslexia and steps they can take to support and encourage their child.

Each chapter is packed with detailed and helpful information, covering identification, public schools versus private settings, and how (and when) to seek professional help. Summary and resource sections at the end of each chapter give quick guidance to busy readers. Topics include a wealth of research-backed activities, nurturing talent and creativity, motivating your child to read, and more.

Offering straightforward, easy to understand, and evidence-based information, this book is a go-to resource for caregivers parenting a child with dyslexia.

James W. Forgan is Associate Professor of Special Education at Florida Atlantic University, where he prepares teachers to educate children with dyslexia and related disabilities.

Noelle Balsamo is Assistant Professor of Special Education at Florida Gulf Coast University, where she specializes in teacher and parent education.

Parent's Quick Start Guide to Dyslexia

James W. Forgan and Noelle Balsamo
With Katie M. Miller

Routledge
Taylor & Francis Group

NEW YORK AND LONDON

Designed cover image: © Getty Images

First published 2024
by Routledge
605 Third Avenue, New York, NY 10158

and by Routledge
4 Park Square, Milton Park, Abingdon, Oxon, OX14 4RN

Routledge is an imprint of the Taylor & Francis Group, an informa business

© 2024 Taylor & Francis

The right of Noelle Balsamo and James W. Forgan to be identified as authors of this work has been asserted in accordance with sections 77 and 78 of the Copyright, Designs and Patents Act 1988.

Library of Congress Cataloging-in-Publication Data
A catalog record for this title has been requested

ISBN: 978-1-032-50995-2 (pbk)
ISBN: 978-1-003-40061-5 (ebk)

DOI: 10.4324/9781003400615

Typeset in Palatino
by Deanta Global Publishing Services, Chennai, India

Dedication

Jim dedicates this book to Peggy Forgan and Linda Johnson: two amazing teachers who gave the gift of reading to children with dyslexia

Noelle dedicates this book to her beautiful and bright goddaughter and her amazing parents

Contents

Acknowledgements

We'd like to acknowledge the valuable contributions from Beth Kaprive, Molly Arthur, Nancy Noyes, and Ashley Rivello which helped make this a better book for parents and professionals.

Introduction

Dyslexia. Even if you suspect your child might have dyslexia, hearing the diagnosis can be monumental news since reading is required for almost every aspect of modern life. You might have a thousand questions in your head. "How will my child learn to read? What caused dyslexia? Will it go away? Does my child need a special school? Where do I find help? Should I hold them back? What should I do first?" and on and on.

Perhaps you've reassured yourself that dyslexia is just learning to read differently. You've seen the news that many successful people have dyslexia such as Barbara Corcoran, Damon John, Richard Branson, Charles Schwab, and Tim Tebow so you have the hope your child will be successful too. Nevertheless, you're worried about what the future holds if your child can't read. We are pleased you found this book because we want to answer your questions and recommend the best evidenced based information for helping your child make the most improvement in the shortest amount of time.

Dyslexia is a lifelong learning disorder that interferes with an individual's ability to read and spell, despite having normal intelligence. While often genetic, dyslexia is not something you directly caused. Dyslexia is not a poor parenting issue. It did not occur because you did not read to your child in utero or early enough after being born. Being a working parent did not cause dyslexia. Dyslexia is a neurological disorder and type of learning disability. Although dyslexia can't be cured, people with dyslexia can become proficient readers and live full and satisfying lives.

This book is about helping you know what to do right away. We offer guidance to help you increase the probability that your child will become a successful reader and accomplish anything in life they set out to achieve.

Sometimes a book's introduction is glossed over but if this was the only part of the book you read, we recommend you take these steps to help your child.

DOI: 10.4324/9781003400615-1

1. Obtain an accurate diagnosis
2. Work with a certified or highly experienced dyslexia tutor/teacher
3. Make sure the tutor's and your child's personalities 'click'
4. Use an evidenced based reading program as described in Chapter 3
5. Provide one-to-one teaching
6. Have one-to-one sessions at least twice a week for one hour per session
7. Stick with the tutoring for 18–36 months
8. Explain dyslexia to your child's teacher(s)
9. Read with and to your child
10. Learn more about dyslexia yourself

It's hard work and your support is a critical ingredient for your child's success. We believe you've got this and we wish you well!

1

Dyslexia Explained

The International Dyslexia Association, an organization trusted by parents and educators alike, offers the following definition to help you understand the cluster of challenges broadly referred to as "dyslexia":

> Dyslexia is a specific learning disability that is neurobiological in origin. It is characterized by difficulties with accurate and/or fluent word recognition and by poor spelling and decoding abilities. These difficulties typically result from a deficit in the phonological component of language that is often unexpected in relation to other cognitive abilities and the provision of effective classroom instruction. Secondary consequences may include problems in reading comprehension and reduced reading experience that can impede growth of vocabulary and background knowledge.

With increased prevalence, research and advocacy, understanding of dyslexia continues to evolve over time. However, this definition provides the most up-to-date and widely adopted language from a globally trusted source and is, therefore, a good foundation for discriminating between what dyslexia is and what it is not.

DOI: 10.4324/9781003400615-2

Now, let's break this comprehensive definition down into simpler terms to help you understand what each of these statements may mean for you and your child as you navigate this new diagnosis together.

"Dyslexia is a specific learning disability that is neurobiological in origin"

- *Dyslexia* and *specific learning disabilities* are often used interchangeably. Dyslexia is a term commonly used by medical professionals and researchers. However, the challenges associated with dyslexia are more broadly identified as a "specific learning disability" in the diagnostic process, both in clinical and educational settings (see below and Chapter10 for more information on the differences between these labels).
- Dyslexia is a "brain-based" learning disability. That is, children with dyslexia are "hard-wired" to process language differently from birth. This hard-wiring specifically impacts:
- Phonological processing (ability to hear and manipulate units of sound in spoken language such as syllables, rhyme etc.);
- Processing speed (time it takes to respond to information);
- Working memory (retaining information temporarily to complete a cognitive task).
- Knowing the neurobiological aspects of your child's learning challenges, can help you avoid informational sources that attempt to oversimplify or dismiss them.

"It is characterized by difficulties with accurate and/or fluent word recognition and by poor spelling and decoding abilities."

- Dyslexia primarily impacts your child's ability to read words accurately (decode) and fluently (accuracy + speed).
- Although dyslexia is most commonly understood as simply a word-reading disability, it is more aptly recognized as specifically impacting reading and spelling, but also

impacts related tasks such as math word problems, long division, following multi-step directions etc. Although this may sound overwhelming, it is promising – as improving in one area may help growth in the others.

"These difficulties typically result from a deficit in the phonological component of language that is often unexpected in relation to other cognitive abilities and the provision of effective classroom instruction."

♦ At its core, dyslexia is "phonological" in nature. This means, your child has difficulty identifying speech sounds, connecting these sounds to letters and words, and being able to manipulate or "work" with units of language. This impacts rhyming, spelling, speaking and other skills that rely on the recognition of sound patterns in words and the ability to recall and replicate these patterns accurately and quickly in the moment.

♦ Dyslexia is NOT a reflection of your child's level of intelligence. To the contrary, a hallmark of dyslexia is the surprising discrepancy between a child's perceived intellectual ability and their inability to acquire developmentally appropriate reading skills, despite receiving more intense instruction than their same-aged peers.

"Secondary consequences may include problems in reading comprehension and reduced reading experience that can impede growth of vocabulary and background knowledge."

♦ As stated above, children with dyslexia often read words incorrectly and without fluency (accuracy of word reading + speed of word reading). To understand the importance of both, consider how it feels to learn a foreign language. At first, you hear and translate what is being said or read "word-for-word." If any of these words are interpreted incorrectly or if you interpret each word too slowly, then the meaning of new words is missed and the overall message can get lost in translation.

◆ Likewise, poor decoding skills and lack of fluency can impair acquisition of new vocabulary and overall comprehension. Over time, these challenges may reduce your child's motivation to read and opportunities to accumulate background knowledge from a variety of reading sources can be diminished. This is not to say that "reading more" is the answer. Your child does not simply need more books or more time reading. Rather, it is to emphasize the importance of timely and targeted intervention to improve your child's decoding and fluency.

Keep in mind, no single definition or description, no matter how knowledgeable the source, will fully reflect your child's unique strengths, challenges, and experiences. However, having a sound understanding of the current state of knowledge about dyslexia at the time of your child's diagnosis is worthwhile. Having a shared language between home and school to support communication and collaboration is also essential.

Dyslexia vs. Specific Learning Disability

The International Dyslexia Association provides an informative fact sheet, titled "Dyslexia Basics" (see Resources) to help parents and educators identify the core academic challenges commonly observed in children with dyslexia. Here they highlight the following core deficits:

◆ Learning to speak
◆ Learning letters and their sounds
◆ Organizing written and spoken language
◆ Memorizing number facts
◆ Reading quickly enough to comprehend
◆ Persisting with and comprehending longer reading assignments
◆ Spelling
◆ Learning a foreign language
◆ Correctly doing math operations

It is understood that dyslexia can manifest in a number of ways, in both the school and the home, that cannot be easily captured in a bulleted list. For this reason, is it important to consider what challenges might be unique to each and what supports are available to you and your child in both settings. There are different ways the learning challenges associated with dyslexia are acknowledged, understood, identified, and described across settings. More important than what label is attached to your child, is what services and supports they receive and where. For this reason, it is important to note there are distinctions between a "clinical diagnosis" and an "educational eligibility" and this distinction determines where your child's challenges will be recognized and supported.

What is a Clinical Diagnosis?

♦ Dyslexia is not a disease, there is no brain, blood or lab screening that can identify the presence or absence of the disability.

♦ The American Psychiatric Association's Diagnostic and Statistical Manual of Mental Disorders (DSM–5) is a handbook providing guidelines that physicians, psychologists and other related medical professionals must follow to "clinically" diagnose a child with a "Specific Learning Disorder" (American Psychiatric Association, 2013).

♦ The DSM-5 was most recently updated in 2013. According to this updated version, dyslexia is an alternative term that can be identified in a clinical diagnosis. However, the diagnostician should specify whether or not the identified learning disability manifests across one or more of the following academic areas: reading (dyslexia), writing (dysgraphia), and math (dyscalculia) (Tannock, 2014). Note, diagnostic labels and criteria are revised often and changes to the process are to be expected over time. A link to the American Psychiatric Association DSM-5 website is provided in the resource section of this chapter.

◆ Not all children who are diagnosed with dyslexia or a specific learning disorder in a clinical setting will be eligible for special education services in the school setting. There is a distinct difference between the clinical and educational criteria that is used in the identification of a specific learning disability, so one does not necessarily lead to the other.

What is Educational Eligibility?

◆ It is important to note that in public school settings, dyslexia is most commonly recognized under the umbrella term "specific learning disability." This term also encompasses a number of learning disabilities in the core academic areas of reading (dyslexia), writing (dysgraphia), and math (dyscalculia). Whereas, one or more of these specific learning disabilities may be specifically named for your child, federal legislation does not require this level of specificity when determining eligibility for special education services in the public school setting (see Chapter 10 for more information).

◆ Whereas, the DSM-5 informs a clinical diagnosis, federal legislation known as the Individuals with Disabilities Education Act (IDEA) provides the guidelines by which public school personnel are mandated to follow when determining whether or not a child is eligible for special education services under the label of "specific learning disability" as well as the procedures and best practices they must follow for children who meet criteria for eligibility.

◆ More specific guidance on how to navigate school-based special education services is provided in Chapters 3, 10 and 11.

What the Research Reports

Throughout this book, we will present you with the most up-to-date and trusted research to help you make informed decisions on how to help your child now and in the future. In this first chapter, rest assured knowing that decades of educational research confirms two empowering facts:

Children with Dyslexia Can Learn to Read

We know that early identification and intervention is key when it comes to reading proficiency, and that children with dyslexia who benefit from a timely diagnosis can become proficient readers (Miciak & Fletcher 2020). However, older children who are identified later in life are also known to improve in their reading accuracy when provided with intensive intervention (Fletcher et al., 2019).

However, it is not just the amount of instruction children receive that produces these desired results. Instruction for children with dyslexia, at any age, must be explicit, systematic, cumulative and structured. Chapter 3 will provide you with more information on what these terms mean and how you can identify and advocate for the quality instruction your child needs.

Children with Dyslexia Can Be Successful Adults with Dyslexia

Yes, there are a number of unique challenges and educational barriers that you and your child will work together to overcome to counteract the risk factors associated with dyslexia and related learning challenges. However, individuals with dyslexia are reported to be as successful as their peers at the college level when provided with adequate support (e.g., more time to complete assignments) and report high levels of job satisfaction in their respective workplaces (Shaywitz et al., 2020). Not only are adults with dyslexia able to achieve these desired outcomes, research suggests they may be able to better capitalize on their own strengths and cope with challenges more efficiently than had they not had the benefit of diagnosis and time spent in intervention for early reading difficulties (Shaywitz et al., 2020). This is both promising and empowering to know as a parent of a newly diagnosed child.

Quick Start Guide to Supporting Your Child

Sharpen Your Advocacy Skills

You know your child best. It is possible you will be the first to see your child's challenges or experience their escalating frustration.

You may be the first to "connect the dots" and suspect that your child is more than just a struggling reader. If you do not yet have a diagnosis, or have not yet sought out the support of professionals after receiving one, now is the time to do it (refer to Chapter 2 on diagnosing dyslexia). Although it is never too late to get your child the help they need, the earlier the better.

The school-home partnership will be your greatest support along this journey. If you are concerned or confused about what support your child is eligible for at school or the progress they are making with the supports they already have in place, document your specific concerns and bring this to their attention. If homework time turns into a daily battle, seek help from your child's educators. Perhaps there are strategies that work well at school that can be equally successful in the home.

Parents are powerful advocates and there is strength to be found from others who have walked this walk before you. Reach out to knowledgeable parents with older children with dyslexia. There is likely a local or online parent support group or a local chapter of a national parent organization (such as Decoding Dyslexia) that supports children with dyslexia and their families. Having a community of parents with shared experiences can be very beneficial when you need guidance or referrals to quality providers in your area. Through strong parent advocacy, there is greater recognition of and accountability for children with dyslexia than ever before—but there is more work to be done. The National Center On Improving Literacy provides an interactive map where you can explore legislation, policy and initiatives related to dyslexia in your state to become a more informed advocate. A link has been provided in the resources listed below.

Stick to the Science

We now have the benefit of decades of research to know what works and what does not work in the vast world of dyslexia interventions. Guard your and your child's time and your family's resources and stick to the evidence-based interventions that will produce positive and sustainable results. Beware of "treatments" or "cures" that are offered as a quick fix, especially those that are disguised as research-based with frequent references to "brain-based" remedies.

Your child can learn to overcome reading challenges, but there is no one-size-fits-all-quick-acting solution. If someone says there is, they are lying. Chapter 3 provides you with a roadmap to avoid these time-consuming pitfalls that well-meaning parents can sometimes encounter in their search for help.

Meet Your Child Where They Are Now

As you explore this diagnosis, know that dyslexia exists on a continuum (from mild to more severe) and the extent to which your child's life is touched by dyslexia may vary from others you read about and will likely change over time. Allow yourself to focus on where your child is now, not only as a reader, but as a whole child. Notice the feelings, attitudes and behaviors that your child connects to the reading experiences you share together. A struggling child is often an acting out child. Attend to your child's self-esteem and feelings of self-efficacy and encourage others to do the same.

Dyslexia can be misinterpreted in your child as a lack of interest, effort, or motivation to read, write or even follow directions. None of these characteristics are inherently true of a child with dyslexia. However, a child who has repeatedly tried their best with little success can understandably become frustrated and apprehensive when asked to perform these tasks in front of others. Without the benefit of timely and effective intervention, children with dyslexia may have less interest, less motivation, and more avoidant reading behaviors over time. The subsequent chapters of this book will provide you more detail on when, why and how each of these skills should be explicitly addressed.

In the meantime, trust your child is working hard and will have the support needed to not only overcome these challenges but also realize their unique potential and make meaningful contributions in this world as have so many who share this diagnosis. You and your child are not alone. Quite the contrary—you are in the company of some very accomplished people! Read about the success stories of famous people with dyslexia who have excelled in their chosen fields and interests including: Steven Spielberg, Stephen Hawking, Daniel Radcliffe, Muhammad Ali, Tim Tebow, Jennifer Aniston and many more in the link provided in the resource section of this chapter.

Not Sure How to Talk About Dyslexia with Your Child?

Often parents are unsure when or how to talk with their child about a new diagnosis. There is no one right answer to this question as age, readiness, and family culture vary so greatly. However, when you and your child are ready to have a dialogue about what dyslexia is and what it is not, there are a number of resources available to you. The Yale Center for Dyslexia and Creativity has published a guide for families to help facilitate healthy discussions. A link is provided for you in the resource section of this chapter.

Linda explained,

> I told my child his brain worked differently and his tutoring was teaching him the way his brain learned to read. I taught him dyslexia is his superpower and since his brain worked differently, he has a different, unique viewpoint from other usual thinking people like me.

Tracy took a different approach with her daughter.

> After her diagnosis we never told her she had an issue or "disability" we just got to work fixing it. We wanted her to not use dyslexia as a hindrance or excuse.

If you are not sure how to explain dyslexia to your child, consider reading a book to your child. There are many children's books that explain dyslexia in child-friendly language or feature dynamic characters embedded into stories that you may read aloud. Check out the link in the below resources for books that may help you learn more together and communicate with one another about the successes and challenges you encounter together along this shared journey.

Summary

In this chapter we have helped you navigate the ways dyslexia may manifest in your child across settings and time and the different descriptions you may encounter as you seek support from trusted professionals. Here, we have encouraged you to know fact from fiction so you can spend your precious time doing what works and are empowered to avoid anything or anyone that distracts you from what matters most, helping your child be and feel successful. The remaining chapters of this book will help you address both the academic and psychological needs of your child and connect you to the resources you will need to be your child's lifelong advocate.

Resources

American Psychiatric Association: www.psychiatry.org/psychiatrists/practice/dsm

Individuals with Disabilities Education Act: https://sites.ed.gov/idea/

International Dyslexia Association, Fact Sheet "Dyslexia Basics": https://dyslexiaida.org/dyslexia-basics-2/

Understood.org, Success Stories: www.understood.org/en/articles/success-stories-celebrities-with-dyslexia-adhd-and-dyscalculia

The Yale Center for Dyslexia and Creatively, Advocacy Toolkit: https://dyslexia.yale.edu/advocacy/toolkit-for-parents-educators-and-students/

The Yale Center for Dyslexia and Creatively, Guide to Talking About Dyslexia: https://dyslexia.yale.edu/wp-content/uploads/2017/08/YCDC-Guide-to-Talking-About-Dyslexia_Final032017.pdf

The Yale Center for Dyslexia and Creatively, Young Peoples Books About Dyslexia: https://dyslexia.yale.edu/resources/tools-technology/suggested-reading/young-peoples-books-about-dyslexia/

Chapter References

Fletcher, J. M., Lyon, G. R., Fuchs, L. S., & Barnes, M. A. (2019). *Learning disabilities: From identification to intervention* (2nd ed). New York, NY: Guildford Press.

Miciak, J., & Fletcher, J. M. (2020). The critical role of instructional response for identifying dyslexia and other learning disabilities. *Journal of Learning Disabilities, 53*(5), 343–353.

Shaywitz, S. E., Holahan, J. M., Kenney, B., & Shaywitz, B. A. (2020). The Yale Outcome Study: Outcomes for graduates with and without dyslexia. *Journal of Pediatric Neuropsychology, 6*(4), 189–197.

Tannock, R. (2014). DSM-5 changes in diagnostic criteria for specific learning disabilities

(SLD): What are the implications. International Dyslexia Association.

2

Identifying Dyslexia

Identifying Dyslexia Explained

> He can't read because he is lazy and stubborn. He can't read because he's not medicated. If he'd just try harder. His teacher was absent a lot so he missed out on good teaching. He's not focused during reading.

These are thoughts or words you might think or hear before understanding your child has dyslexia. Parents and teachers might point fingers at each other or even your child to try and explain reading difficulties. These statements miss the root cause of your child's difficulty: dyslexia.

Your child might already have a dyslexia diagnosis or perhaps you suspect dyslexia even though it has not been formally diagnosed. Smart children who struggle learning to read are at high risk for having dyslexia. While some professionals advise a wait and see approach, we recommend you follow your instinct and if you have concerns, don't wait. Have your child tested for dyslexia. Early recognition and support are key and time is too valuable to let pass by hoping your child's reading will improve.

Although no one warning sign signals dyslexia, several warning signs sound an alarm that something is amiss and requires attention. These are classic warning signs of dyslexia.

DOI: 10.4324/9781003400615-3

Early Age Dyslexia Warning Signs

◆ A family member with dyslexia or a history or reading difficulty
◆ Having more than one ear infection per three months
◆ Requiring ear tubes
◆ Speech delays
◆ Difficulty learning to clearly articulate sounds
◆ Difficulty remembering the names of letters
◆ Difficulty hearing the difference between sounds such as m and n or j and ch

Elementary Age Dyslexia Warning Signs

◆ Reversing letters or numbers in 2nd Grade and onward
◆ Slow choppy reading
◆ Guessing at the word based on the first letter(s)
◆ Relies on or guesses based on pictures in the book
◆ Difficulty reading math word problems
◆ Problems pronouncing unfamiliar words in science or history
◆ Poor spelling in everyday writing
◆ Have messy handwriting
◆ Forgetting or skipping the little words: in, of, the
◆ Having the "word on the tip of your tongue" phenomena and can't get it out
◆ Problems memorizing multiplication facts
◆ Runs away or hides when it's time to read at home
◆ Difficulty remembering the months of the year in order
◆ Problems remembering first names of people

Secondary Age Dyslexia Warning Signs

◆ Poor grades
◆ Avoids reading textbook material
◆ Complains of mental fatigue when reading
◆ Prefers to listen to books on audio or watch a movie of the book
◆ Does not like to read for pleasure

◆ Anxiety about reading aloud and being embarrassed in front of peers
◆ Skipping classes
◆ Difficulty learning a foreign language

Testing for Dyslexia

A dyslexia diagnosis provides a label to help others understand your child's needs but it does not define your child. Your child always comes before the dyslexia. Thus, when explaining dyslexia to others try to keep your child first and say, "My child has dyslexia" rather than "I have a dyslexic child."

We recommend you have a licensed professional test your child for dyslexia as unlicensed "educator diagnosticians" or "dyslexia specialists" results might not be accepted by your child's school. In addition, dyslexia is not a medical condition so most general pediatricians do not test children for dyslexia. Some professionals that test children for dyslexia include:

◆ School neuropsychologists
◆ School psychologists
◆ Clinical neuropsychologists
◆ Clinical psychologists
◆ Developmental pediatrician
◆ Speech and language therapist

The resources section has websites for locating these types of professionals.

There is not one definitive test for dyslexia so professionals use a battery of tests to diagnose dyslexia. In his book, *Neuropsychology of Reading Disorders: Diagnosis and Intervention Workbook,* Dr. Steven Feifer provides an outline for a 90-minute dyslexia evaluation. He provides global areas to assess as well as specific test recommendations. Dr. Feifer recommends in addition to obtaining a thorough family history, assessing the global areas of:

◆ Intelligence
◆ Phonological awareness

- ◆ Rapid naming tests
- ◆ Verbal memory tests
- ◆ Naming subtests
- ◆ Visual spatial skills
- ◆ Set shifting and attention

Shaywitz and Shaywitz recommend this basic battery of tests in their 2022 book, *Overcoming Dyslexia*:

- ◆ IQ test
- ◆ Reading real words
- ◆ Reading made up (nonsense) words
- ◆ Reading fluency
- ◆ Oral reading of both single words and connected texts
- ◆ Phonological processing
- ◆ Vocabulary
- ◆ Reading comprehension
- ◆ Math calculation and word problems
- ◆ Others depending on the child's history

Currently, 42 states have dyslexia laws and the International Dyslexia Association has an interactive legislative map on their website. Many states, such as Texas and Tennessee, are proactive in supporting students with dyslexia and have their own handbook on dyslexia evaluation procedures. See the resources section for information on the International Dyslexia Association, Texas Dyslexia Handbook, and the Tennessee Dyslexia Resource Guide.

What the Research Reports

Researchers are still learning about the brain and dyslexia. What researchers report is that dyslexia is highly genetic so if dyslexia is in your family tree, your children are at greater risk for developing dyslexia. This was reported by Pennington in his chapter on genetics and dyslexia with citations confirming this all the way back to 1905.

More recently the genetic link for dyslexia was documented in the Colorado family reading twin studies by Defries and Baker (1983), DeFries and colleagues (1987), and Fisher and DeFries (2002). They tested 1044 individuals from 250 families and documented the familial nature of dyslexia but no one cause for dyslexia was identified.

Similar findings were reported by Vogler and colleagues (1985):

> there is a considerable increase in the risk for a child to develop reading disability if a parent reports a difficulty in learning to read. Somewhat surprisingly, the sex of the parent reporting reading difficulties does not appear to be a factor in the increase of risk for a child.
>
> (p. 420)

Francks and colleagues (2002) noted that in twin studies, 30–70% of the variance was to genetics whereas Lubs and colleagues studied 11 three generational families with dyslexia and reported dyslexia inheritance was greater than 90%. In the Lubs study there was also a high frequency of ADHD and symptoms of depression. Lubs found no significant differences in income, years of education, marital status, or drug use between the dyslexic and nondyslexic individuals.

Genetic research is identifying specific chromosomes that prenatally influence brain development toward dyslexia. In their summary, Peterson and Pennington (2012) report:

> The main advance in the genetics of dyslexia since the previous Lancet review has been the identification of six candidate genes (DYX1C1 in the DYX1 locus on chromosome 15q21; DCDC2 and KIAA0319 in the DYX2 locus on chromosome 6p21; C2Orf3 and MRPL19 in the DYX3 locus on chromosome 2p16-p15; and ROBO1 in the DYX5 locus on chromosome 3p12-q12) and studies of their role in brain development.
>
> (p. 8)

Much dyslexia research awaits in the area of genetics.

Dyslexia and the Brain

Our entire brain is involved in reading and there is no specific 'reading center' location within the brain. Our genetic differences in the brain make learning to read challenging for children with dyslexia. Simply put, children with dyslexia, at no fault of their own, must work much harder to learn how to read.

Neuroimaging studies have examined brain anatomy and function of people with and without dyslexia using functional magnetic resonance imaging (fMRI). These studies show where the brain energy occurs and identify the areas nondyslexics use for speech, language processing, and reading are in the left hemisphere. Yet, people with dyslexia use more of the right side of the brain in reading. There is professional consensus that the right side of the brain (right hemisphere) processes the big picture, visually sees how parts fit together, help us reason to determine the relationships, and contributes to attention and memory. Our left hemisphere is more logical, analytical, and language based.

Most young children learning to read initially use both hemispheres as they learn to read but gradually a shift occurs whereas the left hemisphere becomes the dominant hemisphere and helps the child becoming an "expert reader." In children with dyslexia, this shift does not occur and they continue to rely heavily upon both the left and right hemispheres. Thus, the big picture right hemisphere of the child's brain helps them recognize the overall essence of learning to read. Then, as the child becomes familiar with the demand of reading, the need for right hemisphere big picture processing decreases as the child must focus on the left hemisphere tasks of greater reading efficiency, accuracy, and automaticity.

Researchers' fMRI studies show these parts of the brain are associated with reading:

♦ Inferior frontal gyrus—articulation and word analysis
♦ Parieto-temporal—word analysis
♦ Middle temporal lobe—semantic
♦ Occipital temporal—visual word form
♦ Broca's area—language production

- ♦ Wernicke's area—language comprehension
- ♦ Supramarginal Gyrus—decoding
- ♦ Angular Gyrus—spelling
- ♦ Herschl's Gyrus—phonemic awareness

As a parent of a child with dyslexia, it's not crucial to try and pinpoint your child's brain weakness. It is important to keep in mind that fMRI studies show that Orton Gillingham based multisensory reading instruction helps children with dyslexia develop the shift to stronger left brain reading processing. Using the right reading curriculum for the right amount of time changes brain structure.

In his book, *Reading in the Brain: The New Science of How We Read,* Dr. Stanislas Dehaene writes, "I am sorry to say that no real cure for these brain impairments is anywhere in sight" (p. 256). However, he explains that with brain imaging studies, after intervention, there is reactivation in the left temporal regions that are close to those typically seen in normal readers. Dr. Dehaene outlined the ingredients for successful intervention as:

- ♦ Intense and prolonged
- ♦ Short daily training sessions over a period of weeks
- ♦ Intense training alternating with sleep
- ♦ Maintain child motivation, attention, and pleasure
- ♦ Use technology
- ♦ Keep children in the "zone of proximal development" so the child works at a level just beyond what they can do independently

With these ingredients, "The majority of dyslexic children thus end up reading adequately, even if performance continues to lag behind that of their peers" (p. 259). Children with dyslexia often continue to have slower reading speed.

Subtypes of Dyslexia

Most children diagnosed with dyslexia are simply given a diagnosis of "dyslexia," but some professionals delve into identifying subtypes of dyslexia. Do not be overly concerned if you do not know your child's subtype of dyslexia as most well-known research based reading programs help multiple dyslexia subtypes. Furthermore, researchers have mixed agreement on the subtypes of dyslexia.

Many researchers describe dyslexia as "developmental dyslexia" so if your child was diagnosed with only the word dyslexia, it was likely developmental dyslexia. According to Peterson and Pennington, "Individuals with developmental dyslexia have difficulties with accurate and/or fluent word recognition and spelling despite adequate instruction and intelligence and intact sensory abilities" (p. 1).

Dr. Steven G. Feifer (2000, 2021) explained four subtypes of dyslexia.

1. Dysphonetic dyslexia which some researchers also call Phonological dyslexia. This subtype of dyslexia is difficulty sounding out words in a phonological manner.
2. Surface dyslexia is difficulty with the rapid and automatic recognition of words in print. These children break every word down into its individual sounds and read very slowly.
3. Mixed dyslexia is difficulty with both reading and spelling.
4. Comprehension deficits dyslexia is when the mechanical side of reading is fine but the child has difficulty with reading comprehension.

Stealth Dyslexia

This term was coined by Drs. Eide. They use this term to describe children with dyslexia who have dyslexia without the obvious struggles so their dyslexia. Stealth dyslexia often goes undetected for a longer period. Children with stealth dyslexia often have a high IQ score and strong memory system which helps them compensate. They also often have strong visual-spatial thinking skills.

Dyslexia subtyping might be interesting but it often does not significantly change your child's treatment. For example, in the Shaywitz's popular book, *Overcoming Dyslexia*, they do not address dyslexia subtypes but rather focus on effective treatments and supports once a person has a dyslexia diagnosis.

Quick Start Guide to Identifying Dyslexia

> The best thing I did for my daughter was first get her diagnosis. This was such a relief to identify the source of her learning challenges so we could appropriately address the issue. The second most important thing was getting her the appropriate tutoring with the Orton Gillingham method that was recommended. It was extra time and money, but worth it in the long run.
>
> (Gretchen C.)

Keep in mind, your child's brain is not broken. It's different, but not defective; it was uniquely and beautifully created. From reading this chapter you:

- ◆ Understand dyslexia warning signs
- ◆ Understand the genetic risk factor that dyslexia occurs in the family tree
- ◆ Know where to find testers. If you can't afford testing, don't delay help. Start with reading intervention
- ◆ Seek second opinion if your instinct tells you it's dyslexia but a professional could not confirm dyslexia
- ◆ Consider involvement in research. Many universities such as the University of California San Francisco, Yale Center for Dyslexia and Creativity, and Tennessee Center for the Study and Treatment of Dyslexia at Middle Tennessee State University are researching dyslexia and seeking participants. See the resources section.

Summary

Knowing your child has dyslexia conjures emotions from relief to sadness. While you did not cause your child's dyslexia, it has a strong genetic link that researchers are continuing to study. Dyslexia testing can identify if your child's scores fit the pattern of dyslexia. Ultimately, a dyslexia diagnosis provides knowledge for you to take the important next step of effective treatment.

Resources

American Speech Language Hearing Association: www.asha.org

Dyslexia Information Videos, Resources, Testing, and Tutoring: www
.brightsolutions.us

Dr. Guinevere Eden discusses Dyslexia in the Brain: https://youtu.be
/8wJRWRpUrCc

International Dyslexia Association Legislative Map: https://dyslexiaida.org
/dyslexia-legislation-interactive-map/

International Dyslexia Association Provider Directory: https://dyslexiaida
.org/provider-directories/

Research Information: www.ClinicalTrials.gov; https://dyslexia.ucsf.edu/
research; www.mtsu.edu/dyslexia/research/

Scottish Rite Dyslexia Testing: https://scottishriteforchildren.org/news
-items/dyslexia-the-evaluation-process

Tennessee Dyslexia Guide: www.tn.gov/content/dam/tn/education/
special-education/dys/dyslexia_resource_guide.pdf

Texas Dyslexia Handbook: https://tea.texas.gov/sites/default/files/texas
-dyslexia-handbook-2021.pdf

Chapter References

Dehaene, S. (2009). *Reading in the brain: The new science of how we read.* New York: Penguin.

DeFries, J. C., & Baker, L. A. (1983). Colorado family reading study: Longitudinal analyses. *Annals of Dyslexia*, 153–162.

DeFries, J. C., Fulker, D. W., & LaBuda, M. C. (1987). Evidence for a genetic aetiology in reading disability of twins. *Nature*, *329*(6139), 537–539.

Feifer, S. G. (2021). *The neuropsychology of reading disorders.* School Neuropsych Press, LLC.

Feifer, S. G., & De Fina, P. A. (2000). *The neuropsychology of reading disorders: Diagnosis and intervention workbook.* School Neuropsych Press, LLC.

Fisher, S. E., & DeFries, J. C. (2002). Developmental dyslexia: Genetic dissection of a complex cognitive trait. *Nature Reviews Neuroscience*, *3*(10), 767–780.

Francks, C., MacPhie, I. L., & Monaco, A. P. (2002). The genetic basis of dyslexia. *The Lancet Neurology, 1*(8), 483–490.

Peterson, R. L., & Pennington, B. F. (2012). Developmental dyslexia. *The Lancet, 379*(9830), 1997–2007.

Vogler, G. P., DeFries, J. C., & Decker, S. N. (1985). Family history as an indicator of risk for reading disability. *Journal of Learning Disabilities, 18*(7), 419–421.

3

Teaching Children with Dyslexia

Proven and Unproven Approaches

Proven and Unproven Approaches Explained

Colored overlays? Special fonts? Glasses? Phonics instruction? It can be difficult to know what programs, devices, or activities can help your child with dyslexia. Navigating the educational landscape across the various programs can be difficult and it can be even more challenging to decide if the program you select will be effective for your child. Dyslexia is essentially problems with word decoding and fluency. To be an efficient reader, children need to be able to read the words quickly to be able to understand what they are reading.

There are many reading programs, some effective and some not effective at all. By understanding what dyslexia is, as well as what elements of a program are effective, you will be better fit to choose a program that works for your child. There is no one reading program that works for all children with dyslexia, but by becoming an educated parent, you will be able to make informed decisions to best meet your child's needs.

DOI: 10.4324/9781003400615-4

What the Research Reports

As explained in Chapter 1, dyslexia is a specific learning disability that is neurobiological in origin. It often is characterized by difficulty with fluent and accurate word recognition, reading, and spelling. Before we can decipher what works for children with dyslexia, some knowledge of the recommended areas of reading instruction will be described below.

In 2000, the National Reading Panel (NRP) was composed of the nation's leading reading researchers. The NRP were tasked to review all of the current reading literature to determine what areas of instruction needed to be focused upon for children to become good readers. Based on the results of this historic panel, there were five areas of reading instruction that were suggested for teachers to focus on (NRP, 2000). By knowing what these areas are, you will be able to understand a little bit more about what children with dyslexia may need in a proven program.

TABLE 3.1 Five Main Areas of Reading Instruction

Area of Reading	Description
Phonemic Awareness	Phonemic awareness is the ability to notice, think about, and work with the individual sounds (phonemes) in spoken words.
Phonics	Phonics is a step-by-step way to teach the alphabetic principle — the idea that letters represent the sounds of spoken language — and that there is a predictable relationship between letters and sounds.
Fluency	Fluency is a child's ability to read a book or other text with accuracy, at a reasonable rate, and with appropriate expression.
Vocabulary	Vocabulary is word knowledge. The goal is to recognize and understand the meaning of spoken and written words.
Comprehension	Comprehension is the goal of reading. It is the thinking process readers use to understand what they read.

(*Reading Basics* n.d.)

Structured Literacy (SL) is a term that is often used to describe effective approaches to reading for students with dyslexia and other students who struggle with decoding (International Dyslexia Association, 2017). SL programs are effective for children with dyslexia as they address the areas of weakness in phonological skills, decoding, and spelling (Moats, 2017). Many schools and teachers use this structured literacy approach when working with students with dyslexia.

The *What Works Clearinghouse,* which is developed by the Institute of Education Sciences (IES) within the US Department of Education, features evidence-based practices for teaching students with dyslexia. An *evidence-based* approach ensures that an intervention has been proven to be effective across a series of rigorous clinical trials. An evidence-based practice demonstrates clear evidence that the particular program or intervention has been shown to work with students with dyslexia. Some evidenced-based programs that are used in classrooms and have substantive research to support these approaches include Orton-Gillingham, Wilson Reading System, Barton Reading and Spelling System, Slingerland, Direct Instruction, and Lindamood-Bell, are a few examples.

When looking and reviewing these programs, they have similarities. Important features of these programs include: (a) explicit, systematic, and structured instruction (b) ongoing practice and review (c) high teacher/student interaction (d) using non examples and examples (e) decodable text (f) and immediate, corrective feedback.

To be effective, instruction must be explicit, structured, and multi-sensory, to ensure the best outcomes for students with dyslexia. Let's break down some examples of each of the components in the Table 3.2.

When comparing different types of programs, it has been found that those that specifically address teaching explicit phonemic awareness on a deeper level have been found to be more effective than other SL programs that do not (Spear-Swerling, 2018). Another critical feature of good SL programs is systematic phonics instruction. Systematic phonics instruction means that students receive direct instruction in the teaching of letter

TABLE 3.2 Evidenced Based Features

Feature	So what does this mean?
Explicit, systematic, structured instruction	Teaching in a clear and direct way, based on what students have mastered
Ongoing practice and review	Ensuring time for practice of previously learned skills and practicing of new skills
High teacher/student interaction	Teachers and students are both engaged in the lesson and active participants
Use of non-examples and examples	When teaching something, teacher shows both examples of that something and non examples of that something
Decodable text	Text in which students need to use phonics skills to decode or sound out the words. Linked to instruction
Immediate, corrective feedback	When a student makes a mistake, the teacher corrects it immediately.

and sound relationships in a clearly defined sequence. For example, teachers would instruct students on short vowels, before long vowels. There is a continuum of instruction that teachers follow so students build one skill upon the other as they master each skill.

For unproven programs, it is important to remember that students with dyslexia need more than just the curriculum they are using in their general education classroom. Many general education classrooms use approaches such as Guided Reading, Reader's Workshop, Balanced Literacy, including Four Blocks Literacy approach. These approaches *alone* do not have what works best for students with dyslexia (e.g., explicit, systematic, structured literacy instruction). It is important that if your child is in a classroom with one of these approaches, that they are getting the extra support from their special education teacher, to ensure that they are receiving a solid foundation in phonics, phonemic awareness, word reading, and fluency instruction.

If you are unsure of something that is in the IEP, or of the program the school is using as well as anything else, it is important to ask. There are tools for parents to find out what types of programs are used in the school. The Literacy Dialogue Tool (see resources) is a great way to start to understand the programs your child is using in the classroom.

Besides the programs that students with dyslexia receive in schools, there are many other programs that are packaged to help kids with dyslexia, but ultimately, have not been studied to support their claims. Programs that claim to correct your child's vision to help their dyslexia are just not known to be effective. Colored overlays are another product that claims to help students with dyslexia. Specialized fonts and paper are other elements of programs that do not stand alone as proven. Your child may like the specialized font, or may prefer a colored overlay, but that alone will not support your child's reading goals and there is not sufficient research to support these claims. In addition, most well-known educational franchise centers do not offer the type of reading instruction that children with dyslexia need. You are wise to seek out a person or center that specializes in dyslexia and offers the programs mentioned above.

Table 3.3 breaks down some of the myths of dyslexia, which should give you some information to help you further decide if a program is proven or unproven:

Questionable Sources

Does it sound too good to be true? Does it sound too simple to work? If it does, it likely is. Understandably, you want to get your child the help they need quickly and do not want to waste any time. However, it is important to avoid profit seeking organizations offering quick solutions that have no evidence of effectiveness. It is also important to know what educational practices are effective vs. those that are mistakenly believed to be effective so you can be an informed advocate and conserve your time and resources.

On their comprehensive website, the International Dyslexia Association provides a list of questions that families should ask when discriminating between proven and unproven approaches to their child's treatment (retrieved from https://dyslexiaida.org/when-educational-promises-are-too-good-to-be-true-2/).

◆ Do the claimed gains in skill development transfer to gains in reading, writing, math, or study skills?

◆ Do the claimed short-term gains in specific skills translate to long-term gains? Are the gains permanent?

◆ Are there independent scientific studies showing the
effectiveness of a given treatment?

Be skeptical of exaggerated and false claims promising an easy
fix. However, feel confident that we know more about what works
and what does not work to treat dyslexia than ever before. There

TABLE 3.3 Common Myths about Dyslexia

Myth	Fact
Reversing letters while reading and writing is a common characteristic of dyslexia.	Some kids write letters backwards and some do not. If your child does, it doesn't necessarily mean they have dyslexia. However, if they are still writing letters backwards at the end of 1st Grade, you may wish to get an evaluation.
Dyslexia is a vision problem.	Vision problems do not cause dyslexia.
Dyslexia only happens in the English language.	Dyslexia has been documented across various languages across the world.
Dyslexia goes away after children learn how to read.	Dyslexia is not "cured" rather students become more fluent and can become good readers.
Dyslexia fonts help children read better.	Dyslexia fonts alone do not lead to better reading, although some children with dyslexia may prefer these fonts over others.
Reading overlays for children with dyslexia will help them read better.	There is no scientific evidence to support this.
Dyslexia can be cured by special glasses, vision exercises, special diet, special balancing exercises, etc.	There is no scientific evidence to support this
Children with dyslexia just need to "try" harder.	Children with dyslexia are working hard but trying is not enough; explicit, structured reading instruction is necessary!

(Source: Understood.org; Gaablab.com)

are a number of reliable informational organizations and advocacy groups that work to dispel myths and ensure research supported approaches are selected over fad treatments. Make note of the resources shared in this book and remain skeptical of those that do not satisfy the questions listed here from the International Dyslexia Association.

Quick Start Guide to Using Proven Approaches for Teaching Children with Dyslexia

So now that you understand more about what works and what may not work for your child, what next? When looking at programs for your child, it's important to remember that they should have evidence to support their approach. Children with dyslexia typically struggle with weaknesses in phonological skills, decoding and spelling. When reviewing programs, make sure they address one of those areas. When talking with your child's special education teacher, talk with them about what programs and approaches they use. Even if they do not have the specific program listed above, it could still be effective if it contains the *characteristics* as described above. Not only should you think about what approaches your child is receiving in school, but if you choose to look for a tutor, you will want to make sure they may be using an approach that has some research support. When you are looking at tutoring, make sure the tutor is supporting your child using some of the approaches above, as you want to be sure it is effective.

Nancy Noyes is a highly experienced Wilson Reading certified instructor having worked 20+ years teaching children with dyslexia. She offers this advice to help your child:

> When you begin Orton Gillingham tutoring for your child, it is important to understand that although Orton Gillingham methods will enable your child to better understand the reading and spelling of English quite soon, tutoring will need to continue for an extended

time to develop proficiency. During that time, consistent attendance will be a critical component in helping your child progress as steadily as possible. While there certainly will be circumstances that throw the regular schedule off, to achieve the greatest benefits of Orton Gillingham tutoring, a regular tutoring schedule should be maintained as much as possible.

Ashley Rivello uses the Barton Reading and Spelling System in her business, Dyslexic Einstein Tutoring, and explains:

It is very important that you understand the time commitment and financial responsibility needed in order to make the Barton program effective. New families should know that instruction in the Barton system requires at least two hours per week of tutoring. I have found that students who do not stay consistent with this schedule fall behind quickly. There is a tremendous amount of teaching that takes place in the first four levels and consistent attendance is crucial to your child's success.

I also let families know that the Barton program can take at least two to three years to successfully finish. Some parents want a quick fix for your child's reading deficiencies and want to get them caught up as fast as possible. I'm upfront from the start that this teaching requires patience and dedication from the parent, child and tutor.

At home, using technology to support your child in reading can be a great tool. Try an audiobook on something they are interested in. Remember, audiobooks are great tools to help children access reading text, but with their ears. Communicate with your child's special education teacher about assistive technology and programs. If they are using a certain assistive technology tool at school, it would be important to use that tool at home. For your child to be successful in reading and communicating socially at home, consider teaching them accessibility features. What are accessibility features? Some of these features include (a) screen readers, in which the computer or device reads what is on the screen, (b) speech to text devices, which type what your child is saying into the device (c.) predictive text, in which the device "guesses" a word your child may be using to text. Your child is most likely using iPads, smartphones, and other applications to communicate with their friends and accessibility features makes it easier for them to do so. The more fluent they are with writing and reading for pleasure and socially, the better. The accessibility features above can really help.

What Else Can You Do at Home to Support Your Child with Dyslexia?

When working with your child at home, it's important to think about what you will do to reinforce reading, not introduce new concepts. It's critical to know what your child is working on in terms of reading. Try to coordinate with your children's teachers about what skills are being addressed and how you can reinforce them in your home. Try to make things fun. For example, instead of having children practice their letter sounds or sight words on index cards, try using a computer program such as Quizlet for digital flashcards. Listen to your child read, in a space safe. Try not to over-correct. Keep your sessions short. If your child is getting frustrated, breaks are critical. Choose books that are *connected text*, meaning they can practice the decoding skills they are working on in a book. Be supportive and celebrate their successes.

Summary

Ensuring your child is receiving at least two hours a week of instruction using a program that is proven effective by research is critically important. Approach your child's school to inquire about the types of programs that they are using. A solid foundation in phonics, decoding strategies, and spelling will lead to successful outcomes for your child. Reading programs that have substantive research that benefit students with dyslexia include Orton-Gillingham, Wilson Reading System, Barton Reading and Spelling System, Slingerland, Direct Instruction, and Lindamood-Bell. Seek private tutoring if your child's school is not using an evidenced based reading program such as these. As you review programs, make sure that they align with a structured literacy approach. In addition, assistive technology tools and accommodations are critically important for your child to use and be familiar with, both at school and at home. Last, your child will make more gains when you reinforce the skills they are learning at school, at home.

Resources

CO-Kids Literacy Dialogue Tool: https://docs.google.com/document/d/1nfa4KbriLwYagEJ4yimM1L-r8lJKP3mjUQSIDjlXDuk/edit

Common Myths About Dyslexia: www.understood.org/en/articles/common-myths-about-dyslexia-reading-issues

Childmind.org: https://childmind.org/guide/parents-guide-to-dyslexia/

Technology Resources: https://dyslexia.yale.edu/resources/tools-technology/

Chapter References

International Dyslexia Association. (2017). Effective reading instruction for students with dyslexia. Retrieved from https://dyslexiaida.org/effective-readinginstruction/

Moats, L. C. (2017). Can prevailing approaches to reading instruction accomplish the goals of RTI? *Perspectives on Language and Literacy*, *43*, 15–22.

National Reading Panel. (2000). *Teaching children to read: An evidence-based assessment of the scientific research literature on reading and its implications for reading instruction.* Washington, DC: National Institutes of Health.

Reading Basics (n.d.). Reading Rockets. Retrieved from www.readingrockets
.org/teaching/reading-basics

Spear-Swerling, L. (2018). Structured literacy and typical literacy
practices: Understanding differences to create instructional
opportunities. *Teaching Exceptional Children*, *51*(3), 201–211.
doi:10.1177/0040059917750160

4

Phonological and Phonemic Awareness and Activities

Phonological and Phonemic Awareness Activities

Children quickly learn our world is made up of different sounds. Upon birth your child hears family members' voices and environmental noises such as the beeping of a monitoring machine, the family dog's bark, or the ringing of mom's cell phone as excited family members call to offer congratulations. In time your child learns your native language to talk and communicate. These are important foundations for later literacy development.

At some point your child will hear you say, "Psst!" since it is a common thing we say to get another person's attention. Think about this word. Without looking at the spelling, how many sounds do you make when you say "____?" You are correct if you said two or three. Depending on where you live and your dialect, you either say psst with or without the /t/ sound. (As a side note, a letter between / / marks means we say the sound rather than the letter's name.) What you just did: thinking about sounds is called phonological awareness. Having knowledge of sounds, syllables, and rhyming all fall under this umbrella term.

Phonological awareness is the ability for your child to hear, identify, and manipulate sounds. For example, dividing words

DOI: 10.4324/9781003400615-5

into syllables, identifying rhyming words, and matching words with the same beginning sound. In its pure form, phonological awareness tasks do not involve printed letters. That's why children who can't yet read can still develop phonological awareness since they are listening and talking rather than reading.

The following are examples of phonological awareness tasks. Imagine being with your young child and you ask, "How many syllables are in the word, bingo?" Sometimes teachers substitute the word "clap" for the word syllable so you might phrase it, "How many claps are in the word, bingo?" Try asking the same question using your child's or other family members' names.

To test your child's rhyming skills you might say, "Listen to these three words and tell me the two that rhyme. Dog, hog, horse." You can then say, "Which of these three words start with the same sound? Pig, wig, pan?" Your child is performing at a more advanced level if they can identify the ending or middle sound in words. "Which of these three words has the same ending sound? Car, kiss, far?" A middle sound example could be, "Which of these three words has the same middle sound? Not, cut, pot?" If needed, it is acceptable to show your child pictures of the items during these tasks. Your child has developed phonological awareness if they perform well.

Another term called "phonemic awareness" describes your child's ability to hear and manipulate individual sounds in words. The phoneme is the smallest unit of sound that signals a difference in words. For example, in the words cat and bat, the /k/ and /b/ are the specific phonemes that signal the difference. This ability is an important building block for learning to read. To test your child's phonemic awareness you might say, "Say the sounds you hear in the word rat one at a time." Your child should say /r/, /a/, /t/.

Once your child develops phonological and phonemic awareness, they quickly progress to the next phase of learning which is that a sound is represented by one or more letters. That's called phonics. We teach phonemic awareness to children since without it, phonics is harder to learn.

Like all childhood development, researchers such as C. Melanie Schuele and Donna Boudreau (2008) have outlined the developmental sequence kids progress through when learning phonological and phonemic awareness. Children developmentally progress from easier to harder in these tasks:

◆ Divide words into syllables
◆ Rhyme words
◆ Identify initial and final sounds in words
◆ Divide words into their onset-rime
◆ Segment initial and final sounds
◆ Blend sounds into words
◆ Segment sounds into words
◆ Delete and manipulate sounds in words

In this chapter we will teach you how to use phonological and phonemic awareness activities at home to help your child.

Phonological and Phonemic Awareness Explained

Have you ever considered your child to be an expert in the study of language or in other words, a little linguist? Researcher Noam Chomsky (1967) explained that as part of developing language, children are born with a language acquisition device which helps them understand and learn how to communicate. Your child's environment is the catalyst for activating the language acquisition device. This helps explain why it is so important for parents to talk to their infant from birth onward. Your child is prewired to learn the language system into which they were born. That's why your child is a little linguist because they detect and crack the language code needed to communicate!

At birth your child begins detecting that others are making sounds at them. Over time, your child should want to replicate these sounds and children typically start by making vowel sounds first such as /eeee/. Your child then detects that the sounds combine to make words and usually around the child's first birthday they say their first word. Children quickly learn that words are combined in sequences that make up what linguists call utterances. An utterance is our spoken words bound by silence on each side. For example, if you say to your infant, "Hi you, cutie pie," that is a four word utterance. In school we are taught that utterances make up our sentences. Thus, in about three years, children progress from being nonverbal, to making sounds, understanding sounds make up words, and our words create our sentences. All of this helps children communicate.

By the time your child enters preschool, they are being taught phonological awareness with rhyming, segmenting, and blending. By kindergarten, your child is being taught phonemic awareness which aids in learning to read and spell. After children develop phonemic awareness knowledge, instruction is often paired with alphabet letters and phonics instruction takes off.

What the Research Reports

Educational research is aligned to support that phonological and phonemic awareness are important for children to learn in order to become good readers. In 1997, then President Bill Clinton through Congress commissioned a National Reading Panel to examine what was needed to help American children become proficient readers. In 2000, the National Reading Panel published its report *Teaching children to read: An evidence-based assessment of the scientific research literature on reading and its implications for reading instruction: Reports of the subgroups.* This report found that a combination of techniques is effective for teaching children to read including phonemic awareness. The other areas were phonics, fluency, guided oral reading, teaching vocabulary words, and reading comprehension.

The National Reading Panel's review of studies found that phonemic awareness teaching was important in the early stages of learning to read and led to improvements in word recognition, reading comprehension, and spelling. Additional studies have documented the important relationship between phonemic awareness and reading achievement (Torgesen & Mathes, 2000). Children with a firm understanding of phonemic awareness skills tend to be successful readers, while children without these skills usually are not.

Researchers Anthony and Francis (2005) reported, "Along with genetics, intelligence, memory, and vocabulary, experiences with oral and written language influence the rate at which individuals develop phonological awareness and the levels they attain" (p. 258). Shanahan (2005) noted, "The phonemic awareness skills found to give the greatest reading advantage to kindergarten and first-grade children are *segmenting* and *blending*" (p. 9). According to Anthony and Francis (2005), children can generally blend phonological information before they can segment phonological information. Hence, these are some of the main activities we teach you how to do with your child.

Shanahan also noted phonemic awareness instruction should be motivational as well. Other researchers documented instruction can include songs and games (Adams et al., 1998). For example, many teachers have children clap when the words have the same sound or knock on their desk when they do not. Using common words in a child's speaking vocabulary can help maintain interest too.

Quick Start Guide to Using Phonological and Phonemic Awareness

Let's start by refreshing your memory about common reading vocabulary.

Phoneme: The smallest unit of spoken sound. The word "pat" has three phonemes. P-a-t.
Syllable: A syllable is a unit of oral or written language with one vowel sound. A single unbroken unit of sound.
Segmenting: Taking apart the sounds in a word.
Blending: Hearing the individual sounds and blending them together to say the word aloud.

Syllable Activities

Introduce syllable activities to your child by saying something like, "When we say a word out loud, the word has parts. We call those parts syllables. Listen. When I say the word cookie, it has two parts. Did you hear them? I'll say it very slowly again, cook-e. That was two syllables. Try this one. Waffle. How many syllables? Correct two. Let's play some syllable games."

Jumping
Using painter's tape, create the numbers one, two, three, and four on the floor. Now make a starting line. Tell your child you will say a word. Your child should repeat the word back and then make one jump for each syllable. You say the word happy, your child jumps to number one while saying "hap" and jumps to number two when saying "py."

Sorting objects
Take four bowls from your cupboard. Then gather about 20 coins or small objects such as dice, bingo chips, or counting bears. With your child say a word and then your child slowly repeats the word while placing a coin into each bowl for each syllable.

Stack objects
Gather checkers or bricks such as Lego. Tell your child to repeat the word and for each syllable stack a checker. If you say the word rhinoceros, your child slowly repeats it stacking four checkers.

Drumming
You might have a drum instrument or use an empty box or a table top. You say the word and your child must drum or tap for each syllable they hear when repeating the word. The word hippopotamus would result in five drum beats.

Rhyming
Pass the rhyme.
You can play this game as a family. To play this game tell your child you will say a word to start, then take turns going around with each person saying a word that rhymes with the starting word. The most common word endings to rhyme are: ay, ill, ip, at, am, ag, ack, ank, ick, ell, ot, ing, ap, unk, ail, ain, eed, out, ug, op, in, an, est, ink, ow, ew, ore.

Create rhyming pairs

Gather common items that can be used to form rhyming pairs. For example, you could have a toy cat and a baseball bat, a key and a toy tree.

Dance

Play a YouTube song with just a beat. Say a word such as can, your child repeats it four times while dancing. Now say a rhyming word such as man and your child says it four times doing a different move. Repeat this process with new rhyming words.

Sing nursery rhymes

With your child sing nursery rhymes such as Baa Baa Black Sheep, Incy Wincy Spider, Twinkle Twinkle, Little Star, or Jack and Jill. As you sing the song, emphasize the rhyming words. You could have your child stand or give a thumbs up when they hear the words that rhyme.

Beginning and Ending Sound Sorts

Ask your child to sort pictures into two, three, or four groups based on their beginning or ending sounds. This is easiest accomplished using a workbook or pre-made activity sheet. You can search the internet for free materials using the term "beginning and ending sound sorts" or purchase material on Amazon such as Alphabet Soup Sorter. You may also use household items or your child's toys. For example, use the sound /b/ and have ten items of which some start with /b/ and others do not. Ask your child to place all the items with /b/ into a pile.

Segmenting Initial and Final Sounds/ Identifying Beginning and Ending Sounds in Words

You and your child can play a segmenting word game. Developmentally, it's easier for your child to identify or segment the beginning sound of a word. Begin by telling your child that you'll say a word and then your child should tell you the first sound in the word.

Say these words one at a time and your child can tell you the first sound in these ten words: log, goat, bird, flower, candy, tire, sink, tap, ring, paper. If your child answered at least nine out of ten correct, move to identifying ending sounds. Say these words one at a time and ask your child to tell you then ending sound: meat, dog, cat, cup, road, kiss, pen, pot, bank, boat. Repeat with new words.

Play games using words that begin with the target letter. Use pictures or common items. For example, show a dog picture and say dog begins with sound /d/. Now I'll say other words and give me a thumbs up if the word starts with /d/ or a thumbs down if it does not. Say the words: dish, eat, deer, dance, cup. Repeat with a new picture and words.

Blend Sounds into Words

Blending sounds is simply your child fluently joining sounds together to read a word. When you tell your child to "sound out the word" they are saying the sounds and then blending them together to say the word. Try these three activities to practice blending.

1. Oral blending. You say a word one sound at a time and your child says the complete word. Say these words one sound at a time. /f/ /a/ /t/ = fat; /s/ /u/ /n/ = sun; /t/ /a/ /n/ = tan; /n/ /o/ /t/ = not.
2. Point and swipe. Gather three or four coins. Set the coins in a line. Tell your child that each coin will represent a sound. You will say a word and then your child must repeat it one sound at a time. As they say the sound, they also point to a coin. After saying and pointing, your child swipes their finger from left to right as they say the word. For example, tell your child to point and swipe for the word dog. He touches the first coin and says /d/, touches the second coin and says /o/, and touches the third coin and says /g/. Then swipes his finger starting with the first coin and ending with the last coin and says the word dog.
3. Slow and stretch. With slow and stretch you say the word very slowly one sound at a time and stretch out the sound. Say the word fun but say it as /fffffff/ /uuuuuuu/ /nnnnnn/ or say the word cat as /kkkkk/ /aaaaa/ /ttttt/.

Resources

Fun Express Phonological Awareness Games: 200 Piece File Folder Game
Fun-to-Know Puzzles: Rhyming, Learn Words & Pictures That Rhyme,
    24 Two-Sided Puzzles, Self-Checking, 48 Puzzles Total.
Beginning and Ending Sounds Splat Game Grades K–3
Really Good Stuff EZread Sound Box Mats and Chips

Chapter References

Adams, M. J., Foorman, B. R., Lundberg, I., & Beeler, T. (1998). *Phonemic awareness in young children: A classroom curriculum.* Baltimore: Brookes.

Anthony, J. L., & Francis, D. J. (2005). Development of phonological awareness. *Current directions in psychological Science, 14*(5), 255–259.

Chomsky, N. (1967). Recent contributions to the theory of innate ideas. In *A Portrait of Twenty-five Years* (pp. 31–40). Springer, Dordrecht.

National Reading Panel (US), National Institute of Child Health, & Human Development (US). (2000). *Teaching children to read: An evidence-based assessment of the scientific research literature on reading and its implications for reading instruction: Reports of the subgroups.* National Institute of Child Health and Human Development, National Institutes of Health.

Schuele, C. M., & Boudreau, D. (2008). Phonological awareness intervention: Beyond the basics. *Lang Speech Hear Serv Sch. 39*(1), 3–20.

Shanahan, T. (2005). The National Reading Panel Report. Practical Advice for Teachers. Learning Point Associates/North Central Regional Educational Laboratory (NCREL).

Torgesen, J. K., & Mathes, P. G. (2000). *A basic guide to understanding, assessing, and teaching phonological awareness.* Pro Ed.

5

Phonics and Activities

Phonics Explained

Most likely some of your earliest memories of learning how to read involve some type of phonics skill. In fact, you may remember singing the "ABC" song with your child, which is one of the first building blocks in learning how to read. At some point, your child begins to recognize his or her name. They may be able to first recognize the first letter in their name and understand that "S" stands for "Sam". In addition to recognizing their name, children begin to identify environmental print, such as seeing the golden arches and knowing that the "M" is at the beginning of "McDonalds". So when do children formally begin to learn how to read? It begins in kindergarten, although pre reading skills are being developed in early childhood years (e.g., listening to rhyming words, vocabulary instruction, etc.). But most of the time, the formal teaching of reading and phonics starts at kindergarten. During your child's kindergarten year, the expectation is that they will be able to identify all the letters in the alphabet. They will also begin to link the letter to its corresponding sound. It's important to remember that reading is not natural. Children grow up learning how to listen and speak, but for a child to learn how to read, it takes much effort. This task does not just naturally occur and children with dyslexia often struggle with the letter and sound connection.

DOI: 10.4324/9781003400615-6

Students need to develop word identification skills that are needed for students to read, or decode words. Phonics is an effective method that children can use to decode, or identify, unknown words. So what exactly is phonics? Phonics instruction, in basic terms, is connecting the letter (grapheme) to the sound (phoneme). There are 26 letters in the alphabet and 44 common phonemes in the English language. These phonemes represent both letters and letter combinations. Your child must learn to connect letters and sounds in words to be able to read. The aim of phonics instruction is to make sure that children understand the alphabetic principle, which is that letters represent sounds of spoken language, and in turn that there is a logical relationship between spoken sounds and written words.

To determine if your child needs support in phonics, you may begin by showing them a picture of a letter. If your child can identify it, it means that they have the first step in learning phonics. It is a natural start to begin teaching your child the letters in his or her name, as well as have them identify their name. Once a child learns some basic letter and sound relationships, they can begin to *blend* those sounds into words. Table 5.1 contains some

TABLE 5.1 Common Phonics Instruction Terms

Term	Definition
Grapheme	Written symbol that represents a sound–can be a single letter (such as "a") or a letter combination (such as "sh")
Phoneme	Smallest unit of sound that is represented by a grapheme
Vowels	Letters in the alphabet that include "a,e,i,o,u"
Consonants	Letters in the alphabet that are not vowels (eg., b, c, d, f, g, h)
Decoding	Ability to use letter and sound relationships to pronounce written words
Encoding	Ability to hear a sound and write it down, using the appropriate letter symbol or symbols. In other words, "spelling"
Syllable	Single, unbroken sound of a spoken or written word. For example, "cat" is one syllable, while "catnip" involves two syllables (cat-nip).
CVC words	Words that follow the consonant-vowel-consonant word pattern (such as cat, mat, sat).

of the most common terms you will hear when learning about phonics instruction:

Phonics instruction has been shown to help students with spelling. Phonics focuses on how letters and letter patterns represent sounds in words. Children with dyslexia will often struggle with spelling. If they are faced with sounding out a word, they will often recall the wrong sounds for the letters. When trying to spell, they may also leave out sound, as *clr* for clear, or they may use the wrong pattern of letters for sound such as *song* spelled as *san*. Children may struggle with spelling simple, common words such as *"said, like, when"*, etc. Last, when trying to sound out a word, they recall the wrong sounds for the letters. Often times, a child's spelling can give some insight into the issues he or she may have with phonological awareness and phonics skills. Although spelling is not entirely predictable, as children become better readers and learn more strategies, phonics has less of an impact on children's words.

What the Research Reports

Phonics is a method of instruction that teaches students the *systematic relationship* between letters and letter combinations (graphemes) that are found in written language and the individual sounds (phonemes) in spoken language and in turn uses this relationship to read and spell words (Honig et al., 2018). Phonics is the most critical skill for teaching struggling students how to read. It is not the final goal of reading instruction, but it gives children the ability to independently decode words. Research shows that phonics needs to be taught explicitly and systematically and in fact, those who were taught in this way were found to be better readers compared to those students who did not receive any phonics instruction or non- systematic instruction (Ehri et al., 2001). It is important to understand what is meant by *explicit* and *systematic* instruction is critical to ensure your child is receiving appropriate phonics instruction.

Explicit instruction means that the lessons are clear to students. Teachers clearly describe and model the concept that is to be learned. *Systematic instruction* refers to phonics being taught in a logical way, with one skill building upon the other. Systematic phonics lessons ensure that new skills are built on old skills and tasks are organized from the simplest to the most complex (Honig et al. 2018). *Multisensory phonics instruction* may also improve phonics skills in the early grades. This approach uses listening, speaking, reading and some type of tactile or kinesthetic activity (Moats & Dakin, 2008).

Phonics instruction using *multisensory techniques* can help engage children into focusing on the sequence and sounds of letters. Teachers can use manipulatives, use hand gestures, and use auditory cues to engage students in phonics instruction. An emphasis on how children should physically form the sounds as they read letter and letter combinations can also support learning of phonemes. For example, when saying the phoneme "/s/" you can show them in the mirror where their teeth and tongue need to be, to make this sound. These strategies have been found to increase memory and retention of letter identification and sounds.

There is ongoing debate in the field of reading in regard to how to best teach children how to read. However, there is an abundance of evidence that the explicit, systematic, and intensive phonics instruction works best for struggling students to learn phonics. In fact, those children that are taught through systematic phonics made gains in both text comprehension, word reading, and spelling (Ehri et al., 2001). Many states have created legislation to ensure that those students with dyslexia are receiving the types of phonics instruction that is effective. This includes explicit and systematic phonics instruction. In fact, all but three states, as of 2021, have some type of dyslexia legislation (Dyslexic Advantage, 2021). For more information regarding up-to-date curriculum and resources, the International Dyslexia Association is a great resource.

Spelling is far less researched than reading. There are no large, standardized testing for students that examines spelling specifically. However, research has found that spelling instruction for students has increased both their reading and phonological awareness ability (Graham & Santangelo, 2014). Spelling instruction for children with dyslexia should include instruction that looks at word structure, word origin, and word meaning. Students should learn the relationship between letter patterns, connection between speech sounds and letters, and should be taught to recognize the letter patterns in syllables. It is also important that children learn to spell words for writing rather than just spelling tests. Children will be more likely to master the spelling patterns of words if they are using it in connected text.

Quick Start Guide to Using Phonics

Remember, as a parent, it will be important to reinforce and support what your child is learning at school. It will be important to talk with your child's teacher and school team to find out what they are learning in school. Your role is really to support and encourage your child to learn this complex task of decoding words and practicing phonics skills.

To start, it is important that you are familiar with the 44 most common phonemes of the English language. For example, the common phoneme for the letter "f" is "ffff" as in "fish". It is important that when you make the letter sounds, you don't add the schwa sound, or "uh" to the end of the letter. To be sure you are making the common phonemes correctly, you should look at some of the resources available to you online and listed at the end of this chapter. By watching and practicing the common phonemes, you will be able to best support your child. Phonics are best taught in a sequenced progression, with one phoneme being mastered before the next. Once common phonemes are mastered, students begin to decode words with consonant-vowel-consonant (CVC) patterns and so on. (Scope and sequence below). The skills below are developmentally ranked on what students master prior to moving on to the next skill. An example of the sequence of phonics instruction for sounds is below:

- ◆ Identification of letter names
- ◆ Identification of letter sounds
- ◆ Consonant sounds

- Short vowel sounds
- Long vowel sounds (such as cake, like, seat, meet)
- Consonant digraphs (sounds in which you cannot differentiate the two letter sounds such as "/sh/" in "sheet".
- Two-letter consonant blends (letter sound combinations in which you can differentiate the letter sounds such as "/fl/" in "flood".

Once children learn vowel sounds, they are ready to decode words by sounding them out. For example, looking at the word "sat" and being able to read "sssaaattt". Before a child can sound out words, they must master phonological awareness skills in order to read phonetically.

Getting Started with Phonics and Spelling
Alphabet scavenger hunt
Take out your child's favorite book and have them search for a particular letter, letter combination, or word. Give them a sticky note or page holder sticky and have them find the page in which the letter or word is located.

Alphabet matching
Have a sequenced printed alphabet ready. Your child can use manipulatives or can write the letter below the printed alphabet. To increase the difficulty, have them match the upper to lower-case letters.

Build a word
Create a list of some of the letters or words your child has been working on. Have your child spell the word out with manipula-tives. You can have them write the word to reinforce the letter/ sound relationships. Make it fun and have them use a different type of writing tool or even have them stamp out the word. You can also give students a series of pictures with letter spaces for each sound. Based on the picture, the student can spell the word using manipulatives or can just write the word next to the picture.

Decodable text

Make sure to give your child a lot of practice with decodable text, meaning that most of the words in the text are decodable. Ensuring students are reading decodable text in which they can practice their current phonics skills is critical. When your child tries to read the word, encourage them to "sound it out" letter by letter and then to blend the sounds together to create a word. For more complex words and for words with more syllables, have your child chunk the words into parts. So for example, looking at the word "birthday", they can separate the word into sound parts "bir" "th" "d" "ay".

Dictation of sounds

Practice saying phonemes, or even CVC words to practice spelling. Dictate each sound or sound combination in the word to get your child to use the knowledge of phonemes and phoneme patterns to help him/her spell.

Letter drawing

Say a letter sound and have your child write the letter in sand, shaving cream, or rice.

Partner reading

Reading texts may be frustrating for your child. Break down the task and have them read one page to you, you the next page and so on.

Point to each sound and word

It is important for you to model for you child how you point to each word as you read. Demonstrate how each letter and letter combination have a corresponding sound.

Syllable practice

Help your child understand that words are made up of syllables and that each syllable contains a vowel sound. Help your child spell one syllable at a time.

Word sort

Have your child sort words on index cards according to their vowel patterns. For example, have them sort CVC words with short /a/ and short /i/ sounds. There are a few variations to this sort. You can also set up a series of paper bags with corresponding objects that begin with different sounds or that may contain different vowel sounds. They can sort the objects and put the objects in the bags, according to what skill they are working on.

Summary

As children become readers, it is critical that they have the knowledge and skills necessary to decode unknown words. Explicit, systematic, and multisensory phonics instruction can give them these skills. These approaches are best help dyslexic students learn to read. The activities and resources provided to you can help you support your child as they master their phonics skills. Spelling instruction and practice are also critical to your child's learning and by mastering phonics instruction, students can become better spellers.

Resources

Florida Center on Reading Research (FCRR): https://fcrr.org/student-center-activities

IES Regional Educational Lab Program: https://ies.ed.gov/ncee/rel/Products/Resource/100679

International Dyslexia Association, Dyslexia Resource Library: https://dyslexialibrary.org/

National Center for Improving Literacy: https://improvingliteracy.org/kit/alphabetic-principle-phonics

Cox Campus, Rollins Center for Language & Literacy (sound pronunciation): www.youtube.com/watch?v=wBuA589kfMg

Dyslexic Advantage: www.dyslexicadvantage.org/dyslexia-laws-2018/

Chapter References

Ehri, L., Nunes, S., Stahl, S., & Willows, D. (2001). Systematic phonics instruction helps students learn to read: Evidence from the National Reading Panel's metanalysis. *Review of Educational Research, 71,* 393–447. doi: 10.3102/00346543071003393.

Graham, S., & Santangelo, T. (2014) Does spelling instruction make students better spellers, readers, and writers? A meta-analytic review. *Reading and Writing, 27*(9), 1703–1743.

Honig, B., Diamond, L, & Gutlohn, B. (2018). *Teaching reading sourcebook* (3rd ed). Consortium on Reading Excellence in Education (CORE).

Moats, L. C., & Dakin, K. E. (2008). *Basic facts about dyslexia and other reading problems.* Baltimore: International Dyslexia Association.

6

Fluency and Activities

Fluency Explained

Have you ever been to a play or a performance and noticed how smoothly the characters speak using rising and falling intonation? Or have you listened to an audio book, narrated by the author, and marvel at how engaging their voice tone is as they read the text? These examples are similar to your child being able to read fluently because listening to a fluent reader sounds and feels good. On the contrary, when a child with dyslexia is learning how to read, they are often nonfluent. They stop and read word by word and may pause to sound out an unfamiliar word. This can decrease reading comprehension for your child because they are using their mental energy to decode rather than to understand. For children with dyslexia, this is often one of the early warning signs that there may be a problem with their reading abilities. You may notice your child is having difficulty reading aloud. Their sentences may be choppy and they may skip words or read without expression. Listening to a nonfluent reader does not sound good.

So what is fluency and why do we want our children to be fluent readers? Reading fluency is the ability to read quickly, accurately, and with proper expression. Children are also more likely to enjoy reading if they can read fluently. When your child can

DOI: 10.4324/9781003400615-7

read without having to worry about stopping and decoding each word, they are more likely to comprehend. Less of their time is spent laboriously decoding words and more time is spent doing the actual flow of reading. As children move up in the grades, the ability to read fluently becomes even more critical as they are reading increasingly difficult text and across different content areas such as science and social studies. Beginning in 4th Grade, a major shift occurs from your child learning to read to now reading to learn. The ability to read must become automatic so your child can read fluently and focus on *the what* of reading, not *the how* of reading.

As phonics develop your child learns to read by sounding out or decoding a word. After repeatedly practicing that word, it becomes automatically recognized upon sight. This is part of fluency, the ability to read automatically. Not only are fluent readers able to read automatically, but they read with expression. The ability to read with expression and pacing, or what educators call prosody, are components of fluency. In addition to expression and pacing, your child must pay attention to conventions of print such as punctuation, to be able to read with expression. Once your child has mastered these skills, they become fluent. At this point, your child can focus on the comprehension of the text. Fluent reading is really the key connection between decoding (being able to identify a word) and comprehension of text. This is particularly important for a child with dyslexia. Children with dyslexia need to practice words they know, such as high frequency words, to assist them in reading fluently. Fluent readers are confident readers.

What the Research Reports

Fluency was one of the areas that the National Reading Panel (2000) identified as being a key component for reading instruction. Research shows that if a child can read fluently, they are more likely to comprehend what they have read. Even though fluency is important, it is often referred to as the most neglected reading skill (Shaywitz, 2020). However, reading fluency is certainly a skill that receives attention via testing. Elementary age children are tested and monitored on their fluency rates. Schools, districts, and states pay attention to students' fluency rates to understand how children are performing in reading and if they are making adequate process towards meeting state standards. In addition to fluency progress monitoring assessments (such as MAP testing), there are national assessments to examine how students are doing across the United State in reading fluency. The National Assessment of Educational Progress (NAEP) assessment is nationally administered in various academic areas to a sample of students. The latest administration of the National Assessment of Educational Progress (2018) Oral Reading Fluency indicated that 36% of 4th Grade students were considered below basic fluent readers (White et al., 2021). This is alarming as children are expected to be fluent readers by the end of 2nd Grade (Shaywitz, 2020).

Teachers often monitor reading fluency by conducting running records. Running records are tools that teachers use to identify how well a child can read aloud as well as any behaviors they may be doing while reading. A teacher will administer a new text passage to the child and the child will read the passage aloud. The teacher monitors the child's reading behaviors and will record your child's errors. A running record is also timed and how many words correct per minute are also noted. Running records are often used in the early elementary grades, as a child is learning how to read. Each grade level has expectations and targets that each child should meet across the school year. These are often called oral reading fluency rates, and they are measured by words correct per minute. The higher the number of words correct per minute, the higher their reading fluency ability. As your child becomes more confident and competent in their phonics and word recognition skills, their fluency will increase.

Researchers have found that in the classroom, repeated oral reading, with monitoring, has led to an overall improvement in reading achievement and fluency. So what is repeated reading? There are variations to this strategy, but in general, a student is given a passage with their teacher. The student will then read it aloud, with the teacher, at least three times. When the student has difficulty with a word or cannot read it after five seconds, the teacher reads the word aloud. The student will repeat the word correctly. If the student gets stuck on a word or needs help, they can ask for help and the teacher will read the word aloud and/ or provides the definition of the word. The student continues to read the passage until they can read it fluently (What Works Clearinghouse, 2014). This strategy has been shown to be effective on not only improving reading fluency, but also on reading comprehension. It is important for students to have opportunities to practice fluency skills in the classroom but at home as well.

Quick Start Guide to Using Fluency Strategies

So how can you support your child at home with reading fluency? Let's first explore some common terms to help you navigate the best ways to choose books and other texts for reading fluency practice. First of all, we want to give children texts that are *decodable*, which means that if they get stuck on a word, they have the strategies to sound out and correctly pronounce the word. Decodable texts are sequenced so that students are reading words consistent with the phonics skills they are being taught. Decodable texts are different than leveled readers and predictable text.

When students are using *leveled readers*, they are reading text that is organized according to readability levels of difficulty. It doesn't necessarily align with the phonics skills the students are practicing and being taught at school. We also want to have students avoid using *predictable text,* because they are not using their phonics skills for decoding. With predictable text, they rely on repetitive text or pictures to figure out the words. They are designed so that the readers use guessing to read many of the words on the page.

Struggling readers and children with dyslexia will benefit more from decodable texts. There are a few reasons for this. When students are given text that they can decode and read, they may be encouraged and motivated to read more often. They may feel independent and confident in their reading abilities. Students also recognize the strategies they are learning are beneficial and help them become more fluent readers.

So how do you choose a decodable text for your child? When you are practicing fluency with your child at home, it should be reinforcing for them. This means that you are not teaching them new phonics skills. You can ask their teacher what phonics skills your child has mastered or is learning, so you can choose books that align with those skills (see resources at the end of the chapter). When your child is just beginning to read, decodable text should not have more than one sentence on a page. Once you have chosen a decodable text, you can sit with your child and listen to them read aloud. If they get stuck on a word, give them a few seconds to try to decode that word. If they are stuck, you can tell them the word. They should then reread the word and move on.

Reading with your child should be fun. You can take turns partner reading, where you read a page, then they read a page. You can also read the page and have them repeat after you. Just a few minutes a day can really make a difference. Make sure to encourage and praise your child. Remember, as they are starting to read, their fluency rate can be slow. Have patience and remember to support them in reading aloud every day. Parents can really make reading a special time to connect with their child. This is particularly true in the elementary grades. It is nice to have some one-on-one time with your child and it is another way you can connect with your child at home.

Children with dyslexia may be nervous to read aloud in the classroom. As a parent, it is important to advocate on behalf of your child with dyslexia in regards to reading aloud in the classroom. Popcorn reading, where teachers randomly call on students to read aloud to the whole class, can be a very difficult situation for a child with dyslexia. It's important that your child's teacher recognize this and that they make the accommodations necessary not to implement this practice. If your child has an IEP or 504 Plan you might want it to say your child will not read aloud in front of the entire class unless they volunteer. One to one instruction or small group reading instruction with the teacher is a more comfortable setting for your child with dyslexia to practice reading aloud.

In addition to fluency practice, students should practice their sight words and high frequency words at home. *Sight words* are words that children can recognize immediately within three seconds. They can read the word automatically as they do not need to use their decoding skills. They also do not need context to figure out the word, meaning they are not relying on pictures or sentences to identify the word. Any word can be a sight word for your child, no matter its frequency. *High frequency* words are words that appear often in text. There are high frequency words, such as the Dolch list, which are words that appear the most in text. Some high frequency words can be decoded and others cannot. When your child is learning how to read, there is often a focus on learning high frequency words to become better readers. You can support your child at home by practicing the high frequency words they are learning in school which will lead to better fluency in their reading. Practice by using flashcards with your child. Keep it short—and only practice a few (three to five) words at a time. Students are even more successful with fluency when they identify their high frequency words in a book they are reading.

Here are some ideas for making fluency practice fun:

Modeled Reading

Choose a book where your child knows 9 out of 10 words in a sentence because this ensures they won't have to frequently stop to sound out words. Seat your child next to you and explain that you are going to read the sentences aloud and you want your child to match your speed as they read aloud with you. You read slightly faster than the speed your child reads aloud on their own. This tactic "pulls" your child up to a faster level as you model fluent reading.

Record It

Have your child record their reading aloud of a familiar text. They can do this on your phone or other device by using the audio feature. Have them do it a few times and they can watch themselves improve with each recording. It can also be motivating to share their progress with other family members or friends.

Echo Reading

Choose a book your child is familiar with. Read the sentences aloud and have your child repeat the words back to you. Pay particular attention to punctuation and expression. As you continue, you can add in using silly voices to keep your child engaged. Have them read the text passage using a whisper voice, a monster voice, a robot voice. You get the picture—mix it up and have fun.

Race the Clock

Choose familiar text for your child to read. Start the timer or stopwatch. Have your child read the passage aloud for one minute. Take notice of any words they had difficulty with as well as where they stopped. Count how many words they read in a minute. You can write it down, show them, and have them do another reading. It should be faster this time.

Reread Favorite Books

Keep those favorite books around your home. Encourage them to practice reading familiar text often. This will reinforce their phonics and fluency skills.

Use Ebooks

Ebooks are more accessible to parents than ever (see Bookshare .org). Have your child read and follow along with the narrator. There are computer programs that offer this feature as well.

High-Frequency Word Memory

This activity can work with sight words, high frequency words, or words they are practicing in phonics. Make two pairs of each word (four to six words) on an index card. Put the index cards side down. Have your child pick up a card, say the word, and look for its match. When they find two words on their turn, they have a match and can pick up the card.

Picture Words

When making flashcards of high frequency words, try connecting a picture to each high frequency word. For example, you can have the word "the" on one side of the word. On the other side, you can have your child write a sentence using "the" and draw a picture to correspond. For example, your child could write "The cat is big." They can highlight the word "the" in red. The more connections your child can make to a word, the better.

High-Frequency Word Go Fish

Make cards of up to 20 different words. Shuffle and give five cards to each player. Put the remaining cards down in the center. Players must pick up a card and determine if they have a match in their deck. If they do, they create a match and it's the next player's turn. If they do not, they can ask someone if they have a card that matches one of theirs. If the person they asked has the card, they must give it. If not, they must say Go Fish, and the player who asked picks up another card. This continues until there are no cards. The winner is the person who has the most matches. This game also works better with more than two players.

Read Naturally

This is a researched-based program a teacher can use with your child (and other classmates) to increase reading fluency. Ask your child's teacher if this program is available to use. If not, request the school administrator to purchase it.

Summary

Children who can read text fluently are more likely to comprehend what they read. Fluency is the ability to read text accurately, quickly, and with expression. Children with dyslexia may struggle with fluency due to their issues with decoding skills. Practicing reading decodable text and activities that support high frequency words will lead to better oral reading fluency. Parents can support their child in fluency in many ways at home and the use of games and repeated reading are good ways to start building your child's fluency skills.

Resources

Reading Rockets: Tips for Fluency at Home: www.readingrockets.org/helping/target/fluency

Understood.org: Sight Word Strategies for Parents: www.understood.org/en/articles/12-tips-to-help-kids-with-dyslexia-learn-sight-words

Free Decodable Readers: www.opensourcephonics.org/decodable-stories/

Ebooks at Bookshare.org: www.bookshare.org/cms/

National Center for Improving Literacy, Resources for Parents: https://improvingliteracy.org/kit/fluency-text

Chapter References

White, S., Sabatini, J., Park, B. J., Chen, J., Bernstein, J., and Li, M. (2021). Highlights of the 2018 NAEP Oral Reading Fluency Study (NCES 2021–026). U.S. Department of Education. Washington, DC: Institute of Education Sciences, National Center for Education Statistics. Retrieved from https://nces.ed.gov/pubsearch/pubsinfo.asp?pubid=2021026

Shaywitz, S. E. (2020). *Overcoming dyslexia: Completely revised and updated* (2nd ed). New York, A.A. Knopf.

What Works Clearinghouse (2014, May). *Students with reading disabilities: Repeated reading.* Institute of Education Sciences.

7

Vocabulary and Activities

Vocabulary Explained

Listening, speaking, reading, writing ... effective communication, in all forms, benefits from having a well-developed vocabulary. In order to understand and be understood, your child will need a robust and age-appropriate knowledge of words, which can only develop through both formal and informal learning opportunities across settings and time. To help your child become a more confident speaker, reader and writer it is important to understand:

- ♦ Vocabulary is important for word recognition (decoding). Children use their knowledge of spoken words to help them identify unfamiliar words they encounter in text
- ♦ Vocabulary is important for reading comprehension. If they have a spoken word to match the written word they attempt to "sound out," then they are more likely to "make sense" of it and proceed with increased accuracy and confidence with their reading
- ♦ Vocabulary is important to overall academic achievement. Vocabulary acquisition is important to succeed in all aspects of the general education curriculum and discipline-specific vocabulary becomes more complex as children advance in grade level

DOI: 10.4324/9781003400615-8

As discussed in Chapter 3, the goal of vocabulary instruction is to help your child recognize and understand the meaning of words spoken aloud or encountered in writing. Knowing how vocabulary learning occurs can help you:

- ♦ Know what to look for to ensure your child is provided a high quality and comprehensive reading program at school
- ♦ Know what vocabulary-rich experiences you can provide at home

Reflecting on your own reading, there might be times when you pronounced all the words you read but yet, you did not understand what you read. For example, read this sentence: "A novel prion protein gene variant was found in the region with the highest exposure to kuru." What does that mean? It's likely you could pronounce the words but did you comprehend the sentence well enough to explain it to a peer or teacher? We must have a rich vocabulary base to understand so unless you had a medical background, that sentence did not make much sense. The same applies for your child. They often can read a word but don't know what the word means. Hence why we want to teach vocabulary.

What the Research Reports

Vocabulary was recognized by the National Reading Panel (NRP) as a fundamental component to the reading process (2000). In the 2000 report discussed throughout the chapters of this book, the NRP emphasized the need for more focused vocabulary instruction in the early primary school years and beyond (NRP, 2000). Here, the research supported the following recommendations for effective vocabulary instruction for all children:

- ♦ Provide direct instruction of vocabulary words in connection to the text at hand
- ♦ Focus on high frequency words that are likely to be encountered across different contexts

- ◆ Repeatedly expose children to new words to support vocabulary acquisition and maintenance
- ◆ Actively engage children to increase vocabulary learning using high-interest materials
- ◆ Use technology to teach and reinforce vocabulary knowledge
- ◆ Use multiple strategy instruction that includes explicit teaching and incidental learning opportunities (e.g., shared and independent reading) rather than relying on informal or singular methods

In 2010, the National Reading Technical Assistance Center (NRTAC) followed up with a synthesis of the research on vocabulary instruction following the publication of the National Reading Panel's 2000 report. The findings reported here confirmed the need for more explicit vocabulary instruction. Specifically, the authors of this report identified the following common themes across the 14 studies published between 2001–2009 (Butler et al., 2010, pp. 4–5):

- ◆ "Higher frequency of exposure to targeted vocabulary words will increase the likelihood that young children will understand and remember the meanings of new words and use them more frequently"
- ◆ "Explicit instruction of words and their meanings increases the likelihood that young children will understand and remember the meanings of new words"
- ◆ "Questioning and language engagement enhance students' word knowledge"

It is well documented in the literature, that a child's home literacy environment with frequent shared reading opportunities is essential to the development of foundational language and literacy skills, including early vocabulary development (Sénéchal & LeFevre, 2002). This is especially true for children with or at risk for dyslexia (Torppa et al., 2022).

Guided play and structured shared reading experiences have both been proven effective approaches for helping children at risk for reading disabilities develop essential vocabulary skills and bridge learning gaps (Gibbs & Reed, 2021). Here, we provide you with fun and engaging activities you can introduce to help your child's vocabulary development while spending quality time reading and playing together in the home.

Quick Start Guide to Supporting Vocabulary

Read and Talk Together

In Chapter 8, we discuss a structured form of shared reading, known as "Dialogic Reading" to help you more formally target reading comprehension skills during read-alouds with your child. Here, we invite you to first reflect on how often you have shared book reading in your home and how engaged and talkative your child is during these vocabulary-rich learning opportunities. When discussing vocabulary, we caution you to avoid quizzing your child or asking them to provide rote definitions of words. Rather, we suggest you use discussion techniques before, during, and after shared book reading to keep your child interested, engaged and talking!

Dialogue in connection to books allows you to determine if your child has the words to label pictures, people, and events related to the story you are sharing. It also provides the opportunity to target new vocabulary in context with books, while your child is highly engaged with pictures and words being shared. To help you read and talk more with your child to support vocabulary development, try some or all of the following research-supported strategies during shared reading opportunities in the home:

- ♦ Choose books with rich illustrations
- ♦ Choose books with the "just right" amount of text per page to hold your child's attention and interest
- ♦ Choose books that are of high-interest to your child
- ♦ Choose books that relate to your family's unique culture and experiences
- ♦ Ask "wh" questions before, during, and after reading. Ask *who, what, where, why,* and *when* questions about what

can be seen in the pictures or easily understood from the text read aloud. "Wh" questions teach new vocabulary by having your child label/describe images or repeat words spoken aloud to them

♦ Point to a picture or flip back to a page previously read to help your child respond with confidence

♦ Allow your child to take turns asking you questions about the pictures or events of a story. Asking and answering questions both help develop conversational and comprehension skills. You can model for your child how to ask you questions and can model how to respond when they do

♦ Adapt materials and questions to ensure they are developmentally appropriate for your child

♦ Keep it positive and fun

Play with Words

Have fun playing games together that are educational, multisensory and enjoyable for the whole family. There are a number of games on the market or created using materials you have at home that will help build your child's vocabulary while you enjoy a family game night. Here are a few examples to get you started.

Droplets app (Apple or Google Play)

Droplets is an interactive language learning app for kids ages 8-17. Building vocabulary one word at a time, kids match words to their icons by dragging and dropping in this quick-paced language game. Children visualize the whole word, relate it to an image, and with fun repetition, learn to understand, read, and spell hundreds of words from 23 topics essential to the English Language.

Outburst, Jr. board game

Outburst Junior is geared toward the general knowledge of children age seven and up. The goal is for each team to call out words or phrases related to a particular topic, such as "name foods found in a lunch box." If their answers are listed on the topic card, the team earns one point, and the first team to 50 wins. It's a fun way to help with word finding, categorization, verbal fluency, and word association.

Blurt board game

Blurt is a fun and fast-paced game for kids age ten and up that helps develop auditory comprehension, word recall, and vocabulary. Players take turns reading clues (definitions) out loud and each player tries to be the first to yell out the right answer. Right answers move ahead on the board and the first to make it all the way around the board is the winner.

Scattergories card game

A category card and a letter card are revealed, and the goal is to be the first player to call out "I know!" and name a word that matches the topic and starts with that particular letter. For the category card BEACH and the letter card S, a player may call out SAND or SEAGULL, or something else that begins with the letter "s" and is found on the beach. The player with the most cards at the end wins.

Charades

Write out some phrases or words that can be easily acted out on small pieces of paper and put them in a bowl. The parent and child take turns drawing from the bow and acting out the word or phrase while the other tries to guess correctly.

Quick Draw

Similar to illustrating new words, Quick Draw is a vocabulary review strategy to see how quickly a child can convey the meaning of a word by quickly drawing it on paper or whiteboard.

Fly Swat

You will need a fly swatter and a large whiteboard or poster board and markers. On the board, write vocabulary words in random order. Or if you're creative, cut out paper flies and write a vocabulary word on each and tape them around the room. With the fly swatter in the child's hand, they will listen carefully as you say the meaning of a word or say a sentence that is missing the vocabulary word. The child then swats the word that matches the meaning or completes the sentence.

Will the real word please stand?

Give the child a small deck of vocabulary words written on index cards. Say the meaning of one of the words or create a sentence that is missing one of the vocabulary words. If the child has the index card with the correct vocabulary word, he stands, holds up the card, and says, "I am _____!" naming the vocabulary word. Use some words that are not in the child's deck, and when they can't find a particular word, discuss the word and its meaning and have them make a new index card with the new word.

Illustrating new words

Having children make pictorial flashcards can be a helpful strategy to learn new vocabulary. Have the child make a little drawing next to the word on an index card to help them grasp the meaning or the context of the word. They don't have to be an artist, but they do need to think deeply.

Acting out a word

Bringing a word to life is a little like a game of charades. The child needs to understand the word in a deep way, so acting it out is particularly helpful to children who need to physically touch or try something in order to learn the concept best.

Boggle Jr

This is a classic word game for preschoolers and older to learn vocabulary, letters, spelling.

Play idiom games

Hot potato. When pigs fly. Piece of cake. An idiom is a saying or phrase with symbolic rather than literal meaning and these often confuse kids. Many options appear when searching "idiom game" on Amazon.

Turn to Technology

There are dictionary and thesaurus apps that offer independent help for vocabulary. Some of these are in the form of bookmarks or small handheld devices. Students can speak the word into an app, or scan the word from their book, and then the app or device will read the definition and synonyms (similar words) aloud. Once a child learns to use this technology, they will be able to discover the meaning of any unknown word they encounter. Check out the resource section of this chapter for a link to websites describing ways you can use technology to help build your child's vocabulary and independence.

Vary Your Own Words

You are your child's first teacher. Consider substituting your child's independent screen time with family talking and storytelling. As you discuss everyday life events, vary the vocabulary you speak to your child. Most people repeatedly use the same words but you can enrich your child's vocabulary by using synonyms of common words. For example, instead of saying, "That guy is walking fast," say, "That person has a lot of pep in his step." Then discuss that when we say "pep in our step" it is another way to say "walking fast."

As former elementary school teachers we used to encourage our students to use "juicy" descriptive words to enhance their writing. Now as parent educators, we encourage you to do the same with talking. We can use juicy words to help our children gain the depth of vocabulary that benefits their listening, speaking, reading, and writing.

Summary

Despite the importance of a robust vocabulary, research suggests that formal vocabulary instruction does not occur with the level of frequency or intensity needed during the formative early childhood years. Here, we have provided you with the information you need to advocate for evidence-based vocabulary instruction for your child in the school setting and the rationale for ensuring this fundamental component of reading is not left unaddressed.

We have also provided you with fun and engaging vocabulary-focused activities you can do in the home that you can adapt to your child's age and interests. Your child is never too old to enjoy reading and playing with you. Have fun reading, playing and talking together using the strategies and resources provided in this chapter.

Resources

Florida Center for Reading Research: FCRR Student Center Activities—Vocabulary:
https://fcrr.org/student-center-activities

Great Vocabulary Games, Apps, and Sites: www.commonsense.org/education/top-picks/great-vocabulary-games-apps-and-sites

Pacer Center: Tips to Support Shared Reading: www.pacer.org/parent/php/PHP-c213.pdf

Reading Rockets, 10 Ways to Use Technology to Build Vocabulary:
www.readingrockets.org/article/10-ways-use-technology-build-vocabulary

Yale Center for Dyslexia and Creativity, Building a Rich Word Rich Life for Dyslexics:
https://dyslexia.yale.edu/resources/educators/school-culture/building-a-word-rich-life-for-dyslexics/

Chapter References

Butler, S., Urrutia, K., Buenger, A., Gonzalez, N., Hunt, M., & Eisenhart, C. (2010). A review of the current research on vocabulary instruction. National Reading Technical Assistance Center, RMC Research Corporation, 1.

Gibbs, A. S., & Reed, D. K. (2021). Shared reading and guided play for vocabulary instruction with young children. *TEACHING Exceptional Children*, *53*(4), 280–288.

National Reading Panel. (2000). *Teaching children to read: An evidence-based assessment of the scientific research literature on reading and its implications for reading instruction*. Washington, DC: National Institutes of Health.

Sénéchal, M., & LeFevre, J. A. (2002). Parental involvement in the development of children's reading skill: A five-year longitudinal study. *Child Development*, *73*(2), 445–460. doi:10.1111/1467-8624.00417.

Torppa, M., Vasalampi, K., Eklund, K., & Niemi, P. (2022). Long-term effects of the home literacy environment on reading development: Familial risk for dyslexia as a moderator. *Journal of Experimental Child Psychology*, *215*, 105314. https://doi.org/10.1016/j.jecp.2021.105314

8

Comprehension and Activities

Reading Comprehension Explained

To become proficient readers, children must be able to both decode written text and comprehend spoken language. The understanding that reading comprehension is the product of decoding and language comprehension comes from a widely adopted theory known as the *Simple View of Reading*, illustrated in Figure 8.1 (Gogh & Tunmer, 1986). Simply put this theory explains that, "children comprehend when they are able to accurately and fluently translate print into spoken language they can understand" (Hogan et al., 2014, p. 44).

What does this mean for your child with dyslexia? It means that an unaddressed deficit in either of these broad skill sets, can interfere with your child's ability to transition from "learning to read" to "reading to learn", which is expected of all children from Grades 4 and beyond. English Language Arts, Science, Social Studies and even Math, require students to interpret meaning from text, whether it is read independently or read aloud by others. In addition to contributing to overall academic achievement, reading comprehension is essential to living independently in our modern text-based society. However, children do not become proficient "comprehenders" overnight or without focused instruction. Reading comprehension is a complex cognitive process that

DOI: 10.4324/9781003400615-9

FIGURE 8.1 The Simple View of Reading.

develops overtime and is dependent on a number of contributing factors. These include but are not limited to:

◆ Reading fluency
◆ Vocabulary
◆ Extent of background knowledge
◆ Knowledge of text features
◆ Knowledge of writing conventions
◆ Motivation

As emphasized throughout this book, decoding and fluency are the primary areas of need for your child with dyslexia and should be the focus of a comprehensive and effective intervention program. However, as the *Simple View of Reading* illustrates, decoding ability alone will not result in reading comprehension proficiency. Whether reading for fun or function, your child will need strategies to reliably interpret meaning from text. Here, we will provide you with the rationale and strategies for supporting reading comprehension in both the school and home setting so this essential skill does not go unaddressed.

What the Research Reports

Due to the complex cognitive processes that contribute to comprehension, both students with and without disabilities often struggle to become proficient readers. One reason for this, is the lack of consistent and focused reading comprehension instruction for all students during the early primary school years (Catts et al., 2016). In a well-designed general education classroom, you should be able to observe literacy activities that are known to foster early reading comprehension and know why each is important for your child. Duke and Pearson (2002) identified the following key characteristics of quality reading comprehension instruction in the classroom:

♦ Sufficient time devoted to reading
♦ Experience reading a range of genres
♦ Rich vocabulary and concept development
♦ Support for accurate and automatic decoding of words
♦ Time spent writing for others to comprehend
♦ Plentiful high-quality talk about text

However, even if your child spends time in literacy-rich classroom environments, explicit strategy instruction is needed to teach your child how to construct meaning from texts accurately and independently. The National Reading Panel (NRP) recommends a multiple strategy package, rather than any one intervention to support reading comprehension in the classroom. Specifically, the NRP identified the following scientifically-valid instructional strategies for educators:

♦ Comprehension monitoring (process by which readers determine on their own if they understand what they are reading)
♦ Cooperative learning (a classroom model where students work in small groups to accomplish a shared task)
♦ Graphic and semantic organizers (visual aids that help readers organize ideas/information)
♦ Self-questioning (readers ask themselves questions before, during and after to check their own understanding)
♦ Story structure analysis (examining the elements of a story ... characters, events etc.)
♦ Summarizing (concisely describing what was read)
♦ Answering questions (responding to questions that requires readers to recall or infer details)

In addition to formal classroom instruction, a home literacy environment with frequent and language-rich reading experiences is known to greatly contribute to children's reading achievement later in life. However, it is not only the frequency of book reading, but the quality of dialogue during shared book reading that results in improved literacy outcomes for children, both with and without disabilities (Whitehurst et al., 1988). Talking about books and modeling "what good readers do" before, during, and after reading can help your child become more proficient and independent readers. Here, we will provide you with ways you can enhance your existing home literacy activities to better address comprehension and related skills without sacrificing the enjoyment of these cherished routines.

Quick Start Guide to Supporting Reading Comprehension

Skilled readers approach different types of texts in different ways. Think about what you do when you first pick up a novel to see if it is of interest to you. You don't flip to chapter one, paragraph one. Rather, you look at the book jacket, flip it over to read the story description, check to see who authored it, flip through to see if it is the typical length you like etc. Before you start reading you have already oriented yourself to the book and have some idea of what to expect. You have likely connected what you are about to read, to something you have already read or experienced and have some predictions as to how the characters may shape up or how the story may unfold. All of this previewing and predicting helps you read for enjoyment.

On the other hand, if you pick up a text book or an owner's manual, you are more likely to attend to different features of the text such as headings and diagrams to help you understand the complex information being presented to you. You will likely read slowly and reread sections that are difficult to understand. If you encounter new words, you look up what they mean to help you understand the bigger picture. You do this naturally because you innately understand that reading serves different functions (enjoyment, informational etc.) and in order to understand what you read you use metacognitive strategies you don't even know you are using (activating prior knowledge, making predictions, questioning etc.).

The main goal of reading with your child should always be to enjoy the experience together and to foster a love for reading. However, you can support your child's comprehension in the home by questioning and observing how much they understand about the process of reading and to what extent they understand the content of what is read. Here we provide you with some ways to help your child learn how to read different types of books for different purposes and some strategies for knowing where support is most needed.

Check for Print Awareness

Remember when your child would hold a book upside down or cover the words of a page with a hand while asking you to read the words aloud to them? This occurs before children develop *print awareness* or *concepts of print.* This is knowledge on "how reading works." This includes knowing that words in print relay a message and that we "handle" books in a certain way when we read. If your child is young or has less reading experience than desired, you may need to assess how much they know about how and why books are read in a certain way. To determine this, you can see how much your child understands the following:

- ◆ Print on that page has meaning
- ◆ Print can be used for different purposes
- ◆ Print is read left to right
- ◆ Print is read from top to bottom.
- ◆ Words are separated by spaces
- ◆ Sentences are separated by punctuation
- ◆ Stories have a beginning, middle, and an end

Point Out Text Features

For older children or when your child begins to read expository/non-fiction texts, you can guide them to understand how text is featured differently in different types of books and how they can approach them differently as a reader. For example, you can ask:

◆ Why are those words bolded, italicized etc.?

◆ What do the headings tell you about what is important to know in this chapter?

◆ What does a caption tell you?

◆ Where can you find definitions for the bolded words in your text book?

Try Dialogic Reading

If you are currently in the habit of reading aloud to your child, you can try to incorporate some strategies into these shared reading opportunities to address comprehension more intentionally. *Dialogic Reading* is a form of shared reading that is known to support young children's vocabulary and listening comprehension while reading aloud books with illustrations. Dialogic reading is an effective and enjoyably shared reading intervention commonly delivered by parents in the home with their children with and without disabilities (Whitehurst et al., 1988).

The goal of dialogic reading is to get your child talking more about the books you read while you are reading them together. While it is primarily an early childhood intervention, the research supported questioning and feedback strategies that are the hallmark of dialogic reading can be adapted for older children who still enjoy shared reading with the adults in their life.

The style of dialogic reading is represented by two easy to remember acronyms, CROWD and PEER. CROWD represents the different types of questions that you can pose to your child to engage them in dialogue about the contents of books you read together. By varying the types of questions you ask, you can better determine how much your child understands and help them use strategies to better understand what is being read to them.

The CROWD acronym is described in Figure 8.2 with examples:

The second acronym, PEER will help you remember to pause while reading aloud to your child to get your child talking about the content of the book. This will help build your child's vocabulary and also helps to build the background knowledge they will need to be skilled and independent readers of a variety of texts in the future. While reading aloud to your child,

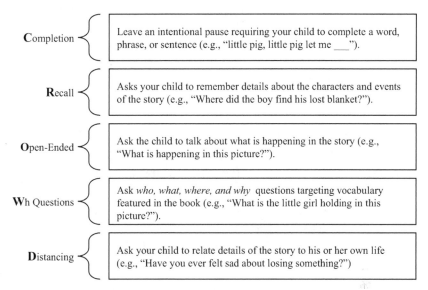

Completion — Leave an intentional pause requiring your child to complete a word, phrase, or sentence (e.g., "little pig, little pig let me ___").

Recall — Asks your child to remember details about the characters and events of the story (e.g., "Where did the boy find his lost blanket?").

Open-Ended — Ask the child to talk about what is happening in the story (e.g., "What is happening in this picture?").

Wh Questions — Ask *who, what, where, and why* questions targeting vocabulary featured in the book (e.g., "What is the little girl holding in this picture?").

Distancing — Ask your child to relate details of the story to his or her own life (e.g., "Have you ever felt sad about losing something?")

FIGURE 8.2 Dialogic Reading: The CROWD Acronym.

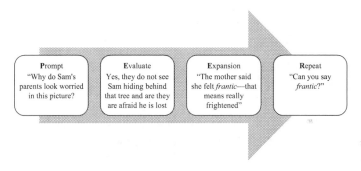

Prompt "Why do Sam's parents look worried in this picture?

Evaluate Yes, they do not see Sam hiding behind that tree and are they are afraid he is lost

Expansion "The mother said she felt *frantic*—that means really frightened"

Repeat "Can you say *frantic?*"

FIGURE 8.3 Dialogic Reading The PEER Sequence.

pause intermittently and follow the PEER sequence described in Figure 8.3 to engage your child in a dialogue about the story.

Asking a variety of questions before, during, and after reading and providing immediate verbal feedback in this way:

♦ Allows you to activate your child's prior knowledge to get them oriented to new information
♦ Encourages your child to make predictions by drawing on background knowledge which supports engagement and helps them anticipate content not yet heard

◆ Allows you to determine and support how much your child recalls about the events of the story
◆ Allows you to determine whether or not your child has the vocabulary needed to describe information in sufficient detail or if there is opportunity to expand their vocabulary related to the content of the book

Encourage Self-Monitoring

Eventually, the goal is to have your child use self-questioning to monitor and support their own comprehension. Often, children are not aware when meaning breaks down and are not sure what to do when they do not understand a word or a paragraph that they have read. Good readers are able to self-monitor their own understanding and have strategies to draw upon when they don't. This is a skill that can be taught, modeled, practiced and reinforced.

You can prompt your child to question their understanding by asking themselves:

◆ Does it look right?
◆ Does it sound right?
◆ Does it make sense?

You can prompt your child to know what tools are available to them to "fix" a breakdown in comprehension by:

◆ Looking up the meaning of a word
◆ Re-reading a sentence, paragraph
◆ Reading-aloud an unfamiliar word or confusing sentence or paragraph
◆ Reading ahead
◆ Using context clues
◆ Using picture cues
◆ Attending to text features
◆ Stopping to ask questions

You can also normalize encountering unfamiliar words and lapses in comprehension for your child, which happens even to the most advanced readers. You can model asking these questions when reading with your child by "narrating" use of them aloud. Keep it positive and natural, rather than instructive or evaluative. Let educators do the direct strategy instruction needed in the classroom. In the home, your role is to help your child overcome frustration and not to introduce new routines that may cause any more for yourself or your child.

Support the Use of Graphic Organizers

Your child may use graphic organizers to help them recall and organize information. They are visual tools that help make complex concepts more concrete. Graphic organizers are easy to make and use and can be customized to your child's age and interests. Graphic organizers used for reading comprehension visually represent concepts such as:

- ◆ Compare and contrast
- ◆ Cause and effect
- ◆ Sequence of events
- ◆ Main idea and supporting details
- ◆ Retelling
- ◆ Character traits

Graphic organizers are a "go to" resource for supporting comprehension across the curriculum and it is likely your child is familiar with using them. However, they may not understand why they use them or how they help. Knowing which are effective for your child and for what skills, can help you help your child use them more consistently and independently. For more information and to find examples of graphic organizers used at different ages and for different uses, check out the links in the resource section of this chapter.

Reading Comprehension versus Listening Comprehension

Most children with dyslexia enjoy being read to even if they do not enjoy reading independently. This is because children with dyslexia often have stronger listening comprehension than reading comprehension. This helps explain why your child can listen to a teacher lead discussion and respond to verbal questioning much better than they can read silently and respond to print questioning.

Parents often ask us, "Should we allow our child to use books on audio?" to which we respond, "Yes." You still want your child to develop foundational reading skills but there are many reasons why using books on audio is beneficial including:

- ◆ Your child has stronger listening comprehension as compared to reading comprehension
- ◆ Your child has the intelligence to understand books that are above his or her reading level
- ◆ Listening to books provides access to higher quality literature
- ◆ Higher quality literature contains higher quality vocabulary
- ◆ Listening to books helps your child understand a book's content ignites our imagination
- ◆ Listening to books helps children maintain motivation for reading and know as they work to become a stronger reader, they will be able to read great books like the ones they listen to.

We encourage you to read aloud to your child even if they do not follow along in the book or take a turn reading. For older students we recommend families purchase a subscription to Learning Ally which used to be called Recordings for Blind and Dyslexic.

There is one caveat to consider. In schools, listening comprehension can't be substituted for reading comprehension. Thus, when your child is being tested, most schools won't read a passage to your child and allow them to answer questions since this changes what is being assessed from reading to listening comprehension. Nevertheless, reading to your child and using audio reading tremendously benefits children with dyslexia.

Summary

The National Reading Panel describes reading comprehension as "the essence of reading" and acknowledges the need for more direct strategy instruction to support reading comprehension skill development. From the *Simple View of Reading*, we understand that both decoding and language comprehension contribute to early reading comprehension and that both must be addressed, if your child is expected to transition from learning to read to reading to learn. Whereas some interventions are more appropriately introduced by trained professionals in classroom settings (cooperative learning, explicit strategy instruction), other strategies (orienting children to different types of texts and purposes for reading, varying questioning, and modeling self-monitoring) are more parent-friendly and can be used to enhance existing home literacy routines to address reading comprehension more intentionally. Know what effective reading comprehension instruction looks like in the classroom and what strategies work for your child in that setting. Use parent-friendly strategies that allow you to play a positive and supportive role in fostering this complex skill during the formative years and as they progress in the general education curriculum in the home.

Resources

A Family Guide to Building Language Comprehension Through Reading Aloud: https://dyslexiaida.org/41523-2/

Reading Rockets, The Simple View of Reading: www.readingrockets.org/article/simple-view-reading

Reading A-Z, Reading Graphic Organizers: www.readinga-z.com/comprehension/reading-graphic-organizers/

Understood.org, Graphic Organizers to Help Kids with Reading: www.understood.org/en/articles/graphic-organizers-for-reading

Learning Ally: www.learningally.org

What Works Clearinghouse, Dialogic Reading: https://ies.ed.gov/ncee/wwc/Docs/InterventionReports/WWC_Dialogic_Reading_020807.pdf

Chapter References

Catts, H. W., Nielsen, D. C., Bridges, M. S., & Liu, Y. S. (2016). Early identification of reading comprehension difficulties. *Journal of Learning Disabilities*, *49*(5), 451–465. doi:10.1177/002221941455612

Duke, N. K., & Pearson, P. (2002). Effective practices for developing reading comprehension. In Alan E. Farstrup & S. Jay Samuels (Eds.), *What Research Has to Say About Reading Instruction* (3rd ed, pp. 205–242). Newark, DE: International Reading Association, Inc.

Hogan, T., Adlof, S. M., & Alonzo, C. N. (2014). On the importance of listening comprehension. *International Journal of Speech-Language Pathology*, *16*(3), 199–207. doi:10.3109/17549507.2014.904441

Gogh, P. B., & Tunmer, W. E. (1986). Decoding, reading, and reading disability. *Remedial and Special Education*, *7*(1), 6–10. doi:10.1177/074193258600700104

National Reading Panel (US), National Institute of Child Health, Human Development (US), National Reading Excellence Initiative, National Institute for Literacy (US), United States. Public Health Service, & United States Department of Health. (2000). *Report of the National Reading Panel: Teaching children to read: An evidence-based assessment of the scientific research literature on reading and its implications for reading instruction: Reports of the subgroups*. National Institute of Child Health and Human Development, National Institutes of Health.

Whitehurst, G. J., Falco, F. L., Lonigan, C., Fischel, J. E., DeBaryshe, B. D., Valdez-Menchaca, M. C., & Caulfield, M. (1988). Accelerating language development through picture book reading. *Developmental Psychology*, *24*(4), 552–558. doi:10.1037/0012-1649.24.4.552

9

Dyslexia in Public Schools

Dyslexia in Public Schools Explained

IDEA, IEP, SLD ... the "alphabet soup" of special education can sometimes be overwhelming when you are a parent seeking help for your child with dyslexia in the public school setting. Like any specialized field, education has its fair share of confusing acronyms and professional jargon! So, if you feel like you are trying to crack a secret code in the beginning, you are not alone.

To help you develop a shared language and communicate effectively and confidently with school professionals, we will begin by explaining what the most common acronyms in special education stand for, and more importantly, what each might mean for you and your child with dyslexia as you begin to navigate school-based services and supports

IDEA—Individuals with Disabilities Education Act (2004)

IDEA is the federal law that public schools are mandated to follow in all procedures related to special education services for students aged 3–21 in K–12 settings. It dictates who is eligible for special education services and what procedures need to be followed in determining eligibility. For those who are found eligible, the law mandates all receive:

DOI: 10.4324/9781003400615-10

- A *free* and *appropriate* education (FAPE)
- An appropriate evaluation
- An Individualized Education Plan (IEP)
- Participation in the *least restrictive environment* (LRE), learning alongside their nondisabled peers
- Parent participation throughout the process
- Procedural Safeguards, enforcing the rights of children and their parents

SLD—Specific Learning Disability

IDEA recognizes 13 categories of eligibility for special education services in public schools. SLD is one of them. For the purpose of eligibility under IDEA, SLD is defined as "a disorder in one or more of the basic psychological processes involved in understanding or in using language, spoken or written, that may manifest itself in the imperfect ability to listen, think, speak, read, write, spell, or to do mathematical calculations, including conditions such as perceptual disabilities, brain injury, minimal brain dysfunction, *dyslexia*, and developmental aphasia" (IDEA, 2004).

- Even with a clinical diagnosis of dyslexia, your child can only be found eligible for special education services if they meet the educational criteria defined by IDEA and determined to need services in order to be successful in the public school setting
- Although the definition of SLD in IDEA may stay the same, the way it is identified in schools may change. A link is provided in resources to help you learn more about these changing eligibility requirements. More information on what to expect in the eligibility process is provided below

IEP—Individualized Education Program

An eligibility label is only the beginning. Once eligible, an IEP will be developed comprised of:

- Present levels of academic achievement and functional performance

- ◆ Measurable annual goals
- ◆ A process for measuring progress toward the annual goals
- ◆ Statements related to special education, related services, supplementary aids, and services
- ◆ An explanation of the extent, if any, to which the child will not participate with peers in the general education setting
- ◆ Appropriate accommodations that are necessary to remove barriers to progress
- ◆ The projected date for the beginning of services and modification, the anticipated frequency, location and duration of these services and any modifications

The IEP is developed, implemented, and monitored by an interdisciplinary team. It is helpful to understand who they are. The IEP team will include:

- ◆ You
- ◆ Your child's special education teacher or a service provider.
- ◆ A school district representative qualified to supervise special education instruction and is knowledgeable about district resources
- ◆ A person qualified to interpret testing results
- ◆ One or more of your child's general education teachers
- ◆ Others who have knowledge or expertise about your child such as a reading coach etc.
- ◆ Your child, if appropriate

In addition to the primary team members, you have the right to bring others with you to meetings if expert or moral support is needed. You may choose to invite a family member who knows your child well. You may also choose to enlist the support of a parent advocate that has walked this walk before and knows how to ask the questions that need to be asked.

504—Section 504 of the Rehabilitation Act
Section 504 of the Rehabilitation Act of 1973 is a civil rights statute that prevents ALL schools who receive federal funding for

educational programs (public and private) from discriminating against students with disabilities, including dyslexia.

- ◆ Section 504 defines disability more broadly than IDEA. To be eligible for 504 protection, a child must: have a physical or mental impairment that limits one or more life activities; has a record of that impairment; or is regarded by others to have the impairment
- ◆ A 504 provides accommodations for students with disabilities to help remove barriers to accessing the curriculum
- ◆ A 504 is how the plan for support under this act is referred to. It does not provide specialized instruction; a child would need to qualify for an IEP under IDEA for this
- ◆ 504 does NOT require that the child's disability interferes with educational performance in order to qualify for services such is the case for IDEA (de Bettencourt, 2002).
- ◆ 504 can serve students with disabilities in the K-12 and university setting. A link is provided in the resource section of this chapter to help you learn more about the differences between an IEP and a 504.

MTSS—Multi-Tiered Systems of Support

MTSS is a framework used in schools to help identify students who are struggling to make progress in the general education environment to help them "catch up" with added support.

- ◆ The key elements of MTSS are: school-wide expectations and universal screening of all students, tiers of interventions that can increase in intensity for struggling learners, systematic and ongoing data collection to monitor progress, and parent involvement.
- ◆ Schools may choose to provide struggling learners with "tiered" interventions such as Response to intervention (RTI) (for academic concerns) and positive behavioral interventions and supports (PBIS) (for behavioral concerns) with increasing levels of intensity until progress is made

◆ One goal of MTSS is to help schools differentiate between students who are struggling due to a lack of quality instruction from those who have a true disability— requiring special education services to make progress in the general education environment

Not Sure? Just Ask!

For more information on additional acronyms you may encounter along the way, check out the link posted in the resource section of this chapter. Although it is important to be informed, do not be afraid to ask questions and seek clarification when information shared is not clear to you.

It is the responsibility of the school professionals to ensure you understand all communication that concerns your child, including evaluation reports and intervention decisions discussed in meetings. Do not let jargon get in the way of your important role on the educational team. You know your child best, the rest you will learn as you go along. Your school team is there to help.

Is Your Child Eligible for Special Education Services?

Schools must follow procedural steps mandated by IDEA to determine if your child is eligible for special education services and, ultimately, if they will require an IEP to make progress in the general education environment. To comply with this federal law, public schools will follow the sequence of steps illustrated in Figure 9.1.

Some important points to note across this process are:

◆ Referral for evaluation can be made by school professionals, however your child cannot be evaluated without your "informed consent." This is requested and provided in writing

◆ You can request an evaluation of your child if you suspect a specific learning disability is the cause of your child's lack of progress. This request must be made in writing

◆ If eligible for one, your child's IEP is revised at least once a year. However, once a year is the minimum not the maximum times IEP teams are required to meet. Anyone on

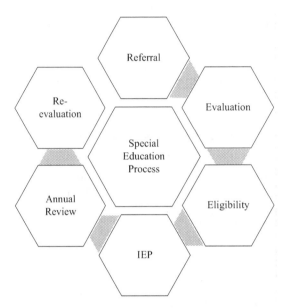

FIGURE 9.1 The Special Education Process.

   the IEP team, including you, may request a review meeting at any time
◆ Eligibility for special education services is re-evaluated
   at least every three years. Although children do not grow
   out of a specific learning disability, they may not always
   require the same level of support in the school setting

What the Research Reports

According to the Yale Center for Dyslexia and Creativity (2018),
dyslexia is the most commonly diagnosed neurobiological learning disorder. It is estimated that 80% to 90% of children diagnosed with learning disabilities have dyslexia (Gabriel, 2018).

   However, the likelihood of being identified with dyslexia in
the public school setting is affected by a number of factors. In a
2020 study examining the characteristics of students identified
with dyslexia in connection to varying state legislation, researchers found that minority students were less likely to be identified

with dyslexia and that the likelihood of identification decreases in schools with higher percentages of minority students and schools with higher percentages of struggling readers overall (Odegard et al., 2020).

Research supports the essential role parents play in the timely identification of dyslexia and the provision of quality services. A 2022 study found that parent's perceptions of the diagnosis process were positive overall. In the case in which parents reported dissatisfaction, it was related to the timeline of diagnosis and the stress and confusion they endured throughout that time. Here, the researchers suggest that parents need more information regarding dyslexia assessment and diagnosis; as well as improved communication, support and advocacy in both the school and community (Denton et al., 2022).

You and your child will benefit from decades of research on what dyslexia is and how educators and parents can work together to ensure children receive timely identification and intervention. However, research indicates a continued need for more parent education and professional development for school professionals to get help to children more efficiently and equitably.

Quick Start Guide to Dyslexia in Public Schools

Know Your Rights

In addition to the procedural safeguards provided by IDEA which is a federal law, a number of states have passed laws pertaining to dyslexia in public schools which may provide you and your child with additional rights and protections. As the result of advocacy and action taken by parents and educators alike, many states have adopted laws that ensure services for dyslexia are high quality and consistent across districts. Additionally, in 2015 the Department of Education Office of Special Education and Rehabilitative Services (OSERS) issued written guidance to public schools clarifying there is nothing in IDEA that prohibits the use of the term dyslexia in documents pertaining to eligibility or individualized education programs (Rice & Gilson, 2022). Know what rights you and your child have in the state you live or who you can contact to learn more. Links are provided in the resource section of this chapter to help you be an informed member of your child's educational team and a knowledgeable advocate for your child.

Know What Instruction Works

As discussed in Chapter 3, it is well documented in educational research that specific types of instruction help children with dyslexia learn to read. Orton-Gillingham based instruction is one preferred method of instruction for your child. In our experience, a challenging part of the IEP meeting is helping the school to recognize the importance of that instruction and having it written on the IEP.

As your child's advocate, it might be helpful if you bring literature supporting the effectiveness of what you are requesting. Share and discuss with the team the benefits for your child. The IEP team might be reluctant to write a specific program, such as the Wilson Foundations or Barton Reading and Spelling System, on your child's IEP and a common rationale is that if your child moves to a different school within your district, that school might not have the specific program. Or, they might not have a teacher trained to use that specific program.

If, through your best advocating, the staff won't write the specific program on the IEP, then you want the characteristics of that program written on the IEP and based on your child's 'priority educational need.' For example, "Based on reevaluation data and teacher assessments, the child can read words with open syllables and closed syllables but is reading two years below expected.

Therefore, the child's priority educational need is to have systematic, direct, multisensory structured language approach to learn the remaining four syllable types (these are key features of Orton Gillingham based instruction). Then your child's IEP reading goals are written based on this "priority educational need." Advocating can be stressful. As mentioned previously, if you do not feel equipped, bring an experienced advocate with you to the IEP meeting. You'll want the best IEP to help your child.

Know Your Child's Goals

Make sure you understand the goals your child is working on and the progress being made towards achieving them. You can use the SMART acronym to help you know if your child's goals are well-written and understood by all members of the team. Hedin and DeSpain (2018) described SMART goals as:

- ◆ Specific
- ◆ Measurable
- ◆ Action verbs
- ◆ Realistic
- ◆ Time-limited

You should receive notification of your child's progress towards their goals at least as often as report cards are issued for all students (typically on a four quarter calendar). Knowing what your child is working on and what progress is expected to look like will help you know if the IEP is appropriate and effective or if changes need to be made. If your child is not making measurable progress from your perspective, bring these concerns to the team sooner than later.

Know Your Child's Accommodations

Accommodations are tools that your child can use to better access the curriculum. Accommodations provide students with dyslexia an opportunity for successful reading. Accommodations alone do not lead to success, but they provide students support so they can learn strategies to become good readers (Shaywitz & Shaywitz, 2020).

Accommodations are designed to help your child overcome barriers. They do not change what your child learns or lower expectations for the work. Rather, they should enable your child to complete the same work as others, but with some variation in:

- ◆ Timing/scheduling (when and for how long work is done)
- ◆ Setting/environment (where work is completed)
- ◆ Response (how work is shown)

◆ Presentation of subject matter (how instruction and/or materials are presented)

Make sure you understand the accommodations your child is receiving and seek clarification if you are not sure when, where, why or how they are receiving each. If your child is old enough, make sure your child also knows what accommodations they receive and why so they can become more independent in accessing them over time. Consider if any of the following are appropriate for your child:

◆ Getting extra time to take a test or complete a lengthy task
◆ Allowing frequent breaks during challenging tasks
◆ Instructions provided in an audio format
◆ Testing in a smaller environment with frequent breaks
◆ Allowing students to listen to audiobooks for certain assignments
◆ Testing students in other ways besides typical text/writing response
◆ Allowing them to use assistive technologies to support their reading
◆ Allowing use of computer programs with spell check feature
◆ Use of speech to text software

Summary

Here we have provided you with a shared language you will need to confidently advocate for your child and effectively communicate with professionals in the public school settings. Remember that eligibility for special education services is governed by federal law and not all students with learning challenges, including dyslexia, will require an IEP to be successful in school. By knowing your rights and the full breadth of support available to you and your child, you can actively contribute to the educational decisions made on behalf of your child and ensure others can see the unique strengths and challenges your child brings into the classroom.

Resources

Ed*Facts* Acronym List: www2.ed.gov/about/inits/ed/edfacts/eden/ess/acronym-list.pdf

Evaluation and Eligibility for SLD: www.greatschools.org/gk/articles/evaluation-and-eligibility-for-specific-learning-disabilities/

International Dyslexia Association, Accommodations for Students with Dyslexia: https://dyslexiaida.org/accommodations-for-students-with-dyslexia/

National Center of Improving Literacy, State of Dyslexia: https://improvingliteracy.org/state-of-dyslexia

The Difference Between IEPs and 504 plans: www.understood.org/en/articles/the-difference-between-ieps-and-504-plans

References

de Bettencourt, L. U. (2002). Understanding the differences between IDEA and Section 504. *Teaching Exceptional Children*, *34*(3), 16–23.

Denton, K., Coneway, B., Simmons, M., Behl, M., & Shin, M. (2022). Parents' voices matter: A mixed-method study on the dyslexia diagnosis process. *Psychology in the Schools*.

Gabriel, R. (2018). Preparing literacy professionals: The case of dyslexia. *Journal of Literacy Research*, *50*(2), 262–270.

Hedin, L., & DeSpain, S. (2018). SMART or not? Writing specific, measurable IEP goals. *TEACHING Exceptional Children*, *51*(2), 100–110.

Rice, M., & Gilson, C. B. (2022). Dyslexia Identification: Tackling Current Issues in Schools. *Intervention in School and Clinic*, 10534512221081278.

Odegard, T. N., Farris, E. A., Middleton, A. E., Oslund, E., & Rimrodt-Frierson, S. (2020). Characteristics of students identified with dyslexia within the context of state legislation. *Journal of Learning Disabilities*, *53*(5), 366–379.

Shaywitz, S., & Shaywitz, J. (2020). *Overcoming dyslexia* (2nd ed). New York, Vintage Press.

10

Dyslexia in Private Settings

Dyslexia in Private Settings Explained

We watched our daughter struggle for years in the public school. Despite being on an IEP, receiving extra help from her teachers, and seeing a tutor weekly, she was not grasping many core concepts and her grades were not improving. Most importantly, her self-esteem deteriorated and many days she came home crying. It was excruciating to watch and we felt helpless as parents. We knew she needed a different school environment but we could not find the right place for her.

We were really losing hope when we found Educational Pathways Academy (EPA). The school was an answer to our prayers. We immediately felt that there was something special about the school when we met Molly. Instantly we knew it was the right place for our daughter. The teachers truly care about every child. The curriculum is designed to help her really learn and succeed. As a result, our daughter has flourished. She is understanding what she is being taught, which is reflected in her consistently getting A's and B's on her report cards. She never cared about her grades before, but now she is motivated to do well. But even better than that, her self esteem is

DOI: 10.4324/9781003400615-11

back. She is happy and confident; and feels loved, safe and accepted at school. EPA has been truly life changing for her. Our daughter has become who she is today as a direct result of her experience at this school.

(Greg and Lori)

After receiving your child's dyslexia diagnosis, you might consider, "Does my child need to attend a special school for children with dyslexia." This is a valuable question since time is precious and your child's future is at stake. It is extremely difficult to make up for lost instructional time and you don't want the gap between your child and their classmates to widen. Having the "right" school fit is a key element for your child's success.

What the Research Reports

The professional literature is sparse when addressing the question, "Which is best, public or private school education for children with dyslexia." The answer often involves multiple facets of life including your beliefs, finances, available options, and your child.

Nalavany and colleagues surveyed 224 adults with dyslexia to understand the prior experiences that facilitated or hindered their successful living. They reported,

Adults with dyslexia who attended specialist schools were significantly less likely to be clinically diagnosed with anxiety or depression, and they experienced significantly less emotional distress with regard to their dyslexia, and significantly higher levels of self-esteem, than their peers who did not attend such specialist schools.

(p. 196)

In Ireland, Mary Nugent (2007) surveyed parents regarding their preferences about their child's education in special schools, resource teaching, or reading units (special classes). She reported, "When the immediate experiences of parents are compared

across the three settings, it emerges that parents are more positive and more satisfied with specialist services than with main-
stream resource provision" (p. 58).

Special schools understand students with dyslexia and train
their teachers in teaching methods specifically for dyslexics.
Shaywitz and Shaywitz (2020, p. 317) recommend that if you are
dissatisfied with your child's public school, you might consider
changing schools if:

◆ The school provided a special reading program and your
  child is still lagging behind
◆ The school can't organize an effective program and your
  child is falling behind
◆ The constant battle to have the school provide promised
  services is adversely affecting your family
◆ The continual lack of understanding is taking a toll on
  your child in terms of his or her self concept and desire to
  learn and go to school
◆ Your child is demonstrating the onset of negative
  behaviors

In his book, *The Dyslexia Empowerment Plan*, Ben Foss acknowledges the distress caused by dyslexia and that most adult dyslexics he knows reached "very dark and low points during their
school years" (p. 221). During the tween and teenage years these
low points can fester into thoughts of death and self-harm. He
recommends that your child's psychological experiences should
be the most important consideration when changing schools
rather than your child's academic performance. If emotionally
damaged, the years of therapy your child might need to heal
emotional scars can be much longer than the tutoring needed to
close the reading gap.

Quick Start Guide to Private Settings

One of the best things I did was get my daughter to a
special school for dyslexia. In public school we had to
reinforce her learning with tutoring 3 to 4x a week even

during the summer. With her schoolwork and afternoon tutoring, she was exhausted. Her special school allows her to be a child. It provides her with skills and tools to help her use her gifts and has brought her reading to grade level.

(Kaylie W.)

Where should you start? First, consider the severity of your child's dyslexia. Most children with mild to moderate dyslexia can be successful in a traditional school if the school offers teaching approaches like those discussed in Chapter 3 to help children with dyslexia *and* also makes accommodations. Children with severe dyslexia fare better in a special school or center that specializes in teaching children with dyslexia.

Consider these points if your child's dyslexia is mild to moderate:

1. Identify your resources
   a. What type of dyslexia treatments are offered in your geographic region?
   b. Are there tutors or special schools?
2. Identify your child's learning
   a. Is your child a better in-person or online learner?
   b. Does your child work equally as well for a younger tutor as well as a male or female tutor?
3. Identify your finances. Private schools and tutors are expensive
4. Does your child qualify for specialized instructional goals on an IEP?
5. Is your child a self-starter or motivated?
6. How is your child's self-esteem?

Consider these points if your child's dyslexia is severe:

1. Are there special schools in your geographic region?
2. Is your family willing to relocate?
3. Would you send your child to a residential dyslexia school?
4. Would you send your child to a highly intensive summer camp?

5. Can you hire a private dyslexia specialist teacher to daily work with your child one-to-one?
6. How is your child's self-esteem?

Molly Arthur, founder of Educational Pathways Academy in Florida, explains three important questions you can ask the principal or headmaster when considering a private dyslexia school. She also provided the type of answer you should hope to receive.

1. What type of reading remediation program do you offer and what is the frequency of the instruction?
    Answer: look for Structured Literacy and/or Orton-Gillingham (OG) approach delivered with integrity
2. Other than OG, how does your school develop reading & literacy skills?
    Answer: Look for answers here that acknowledge that OG is a vital piece, but that students also need instruction in the development of fluency, comprehension, and language development
3. How will your school be deliberately different from all the others we have tried?
    Answer: Look for answers that put the child's needs first and indicate a deep understanding of students with learning differences …
    Small group instruction
    Targeted instructional groups
    Built in accommodations (no fight needed)
    Frequent breaks, gum and fidgets allowed
    Opportunities for challenge and maximizing strengths
    Language development in every classroom
    Curriculum that supports best practices for students with dyslexia
    Evidence that leadership is completely committed to the mission and recognizes the truly amazing qualities students with dyslexia possess.
    Parents should look for confirmation that their child's weaknesses will be addressed properly, yet that the

school sees their child as much more than his/her weaknesses

Ultimately, given your resources and the available dyslexia resources, you'll do what you believe is best for your child. Remember, doing something is better than doing nothing or taking a hope it gets better and let's see approach. As one parent told us, "A short-term sacrifice of money and time can result in huge dividends for your child's future."

Dyslexia Summer Camps

There are residential summer camps for children with dyslexia. One of the most well-known is Camp Spring Creek founded in 2003 by Susie and Steve van der Vorst. Located in the western North Carolina mountains, they are an International Dyslexia Association accredited camp for children ages seven to 15. Campers receive daily one-to-one tutoring using the Orton-Gillingham method. They also receive one hour of daily oral reading with a staff member as well as typing and a study hall. Campers experience fun with activities such as hiking, rock climbing, ziplining, paintball, yoga, and river rafting.

In Kentucky, Potters Ranch dyslexia camp offers an Orton-Gillingham based approach to help children with dyslexia ages six to 17 to improve their reading. Campers receive daily one-to-one tutoring, typing, fluency, and study hall intermixed with fun activities in art, science, and robotics. Potters Ranch also offers horsemanship, ziplining, sports, and performing arts offerings.

Private Schools for Dyslexia

There are many high quality private and independent schools for children with dyslexia. You'll find many below and, given space limitations, we included a short description for select schools. An internet search might reveal schools in your geographic area.

Arizona

♦ The Jones-Gordon School, https://jonesgordon.org, offers a daily flex program in the child's area of need. They

serve students who have dyslexia and related learning differences in Grades 1–12
- The New Way Academy, https://newwayacademy.org, is Grades 1–12 and each student's curriculum is planned around educational needs and abilities based on thorough academic, psycho-educational, speech and language and motor skills assessments
- Pathways School, www.pathwaysschool.org

California

- Park Century School, www.parkcenturyschool.org, serves children in Grades 1–8 who have had neuropsychological testing revealing an average to superior intellect as well as language-based learning challenges. Their program utilizes the latest research on brain plasticity and neurodiversity to help remediate the student's academic struggles
- The Prentice School, www.prentice.org, began with the goal to create "an educational institution that would give children with dyslexia the education they deserved." They serve students through 8th Grade using a multisensory, Orton-Gillingham approach to instruction. The school has onsite speech-language therapists as well as occupational therapists
- Charles Armstrong School: www.charlesarmstrong.org
- Westmark School: www.westmarkschool.org

Connecticut
- Eagle Hill School: www.eaglehillschool.org
- Forman School: www.formanschool.org
- Southport School: www.southportschool.org
- Villa Maria School: http://villamariaschool.org

Florida
- Educational Pathways Academy, www.educational pathwaysacademy.com, is a school for students Grades 1–11 with language-based learning disabilities, such as

dyslexia. It has campuses in Ft. Myers and Naples. Their approach to learning was designed to address the needs and challenges of students with dyslexia using proven methods and approaches such as Orton-Gillingham

◆ The Bilgrav School, www.bilgravschool.org, specializes in one-to-one daily Orton Gillingham instruction and a multisensory curriculum for dyslexic students in the first through 8th grade

◆ The Roberts Academy, www.flsouthern.edu/roberts-academy/home.aspx, provides a full complement of academic programs for students in addition to support and training for parents and teachers of students with dyslexia in Grades 2–8

◆ Depaul School: www.depaulschool.com

◆ Tampa Day School: www.tampadayschool.com

◆ McGlannan School: www.mcglannanschool.com

Georgia

◆ The Schenck School, www.schenck.org, is located in Atlanta, Georgia. They serve students in kindergarten–6th Grade. Their strategy is "the focused, accelerated remediation of dyslexia using the Orton-Gillingham approach" with the goal to help children `prepare to reenter mainstream schools successfully"

◆ Grace Point School: www.gracepointschool.org

◆ Sage School: www.sageschool.net

◆ Atlanta Speech School: www.atlantaspeechschool.org

Illinois

◆ Brehm Preparatory School: www.brehm.org

◆ The Cove School: www.coveschool.org

Kentucky

◆ The de Paul School: www.depaulschool.org

Louisiana

◆ The Louisiana Key Academy, www.lkaschools.com, uses evidenced based curriculum to create opportunities for children to learn through the "lens of dyslexia" using multiple modality and interdisciplinary methods of instruction

Maryland

- ◆ The Highlands School: www.highlandsschool.net
- ◆ The Jemicy School, https://jemicyschool.org, is accredited by the International Dyslexia Association (IDA) and has been educating students with dyslexia or other related language-based learning differences since 1973. They and serve students in Grades 1–12 through multisensory, research-based programs and techniques
- ◆ The Odyssey School: www.theodysseyschool.org
- ◆ The Siena School: www.thesienaschool.org
- ◆ Summit School: thesummitschool.org

Massachusetts

- ◆ The Carroll School: www.carrollschool.org
- ◆ The Landmark School, www.landmarkschool.org, serves students Grades 2–12 with dyslexia or other language-based learning disabilities through daily, personalized, one-on-one tutoring and small class sizes

Michigan

- ◆ Ann Arbor Academy: www.annarboracademy.org
- ◆ Lake Michigan Academy: www.lakemichiganacademy.org

Missouri

- ◆ Churchill Center and School: www.churchillstl.org
- ◆ Miriam School: www.miriamstl.org

New York

- ◆ The Gow School: www.gow.org
- ◆ The Kildonan School, www.kildonan.org, is a private boarding and day school. They serve students with dyslexia or language-based learning differences by offering daily one-to-one Orton-Gillingham language remediation as well as a college preparatory curriculum

- Parkside School: www.parksideschool.org
- The Shefta School, www.shefaschool.org, is a Jewish day school serving students in Grades 1–8 who have language-based learning disabilities. The school uses the following curriculum tools: PAF (and Orton-Gillingham reading program), the Hochman Method (a writing program) and Multisensory Math. It was noted that, "speech-language and occupational therapy are embedded into the class-rooms and curriculum"
- Sterling School: www.sterlingschool.com
- The Winward School: www.thewindwardschool.org

New Jersey

- Banyan School: https://banyanschool.org
- The Craig School: www.craigschool.org
- Newgrange School: www.thenewgrange.org
- The Lewis School of Princeton: www.lewisschool.org
- The Winston School: www.winstonschool.org

North Carolina

- Carolina Day Key School: www.carolinaday.org/academics/key-school
- Fletcher Academy: www.tfaraleigh.org
- Noble Academy: www.nobleknights.org
- Summit School: www.summitschool.com/the-student-experience/triad-academy

Ohio

- Lawrence School: www.lawrenceschool.org
- Marburn Academy: www.marburnacademy.org

Oregon

- Edison High School: www.edisonhs.org

South Carolina

- The Trident Academy, https://tridentacademy.com, is one of only 18 schools nationwide accredited by the Academy of Orton-Gillingham Practitioners and

Educators. They serve students in Grades K–12 through the use of multi-sensory and research-based teaching approaches including Orton-Gillingham and project-based learning

Tennessee
♦ Bodine School: https://bodineschool.org

Texas
♦ Briarwood School: www.briarwoodschool.org
♦ Dallas Academy: www.dallas-academy.com
♦ Hill School: www.hillschool.org
♦ Hillier School: www.hillierschool.org
♦ Oak Hill Academy: https://oakhillacademy.org

Virginia
♦ The Oakwood School, www.oakwoodschool.com, uses a research-based phonetic reading program as well as a multisensory education program in Grades 1–8
♦ Chesapeake Bay Academy: www.cba-va.org

Washington
♦ The Hamlin Robinson School, www.hamlinrobinson.org, specializes in programs for students, whose primary learning challenge is dyslexia and related language-based difficulties. They incorporate a multisensory language approach in their academic curriculum and students are accepted based upon their instructional level

Washington DC
♦ The Lab School, www.labschool.org, serves students in Grades 1–12 who have language-based learning differences, such as dyslexia through the use of an innovative, multi-sensory, experiential arts-centered curriculum. The school has four divisions: a lower school, middle school, upper school as well as a global division

Summary

You have the greatest understanding of your family and child so what is your parental instinct telling you about your child's school placement? In our experience, a parent's instinct is highly accurate. Dyslexia tutors and schools provide an understanding place for your child to feel comfortable and take academic risks needed for growth. If your child believes they will be made fun of, ridiculed, or bullied for their reading deficits, they will not take the risk of looking dumb. Having the right school fit can help or hinder your child academically and psychologically. You know best if attending a special summer camp right for your child.

Resources

Potters Ranch Camp (KY): http://quest.pottersranch.org/about/dyslexia.php

Camp Spring Creek (NC): http://campspringcreek.org

Chapter References

Foss, B. (2013). *The dyslexia empowerment plan: A blueprint for renewing your child's confidence and love of learning*. Ballantine Books.

Nalavany, B. A., Carawan, L. W., & Brown, L. J. (2011). Considering the role of traditional and specialist schools: Do school experiences impact the emotional well-being and self-esteem of adults with dyslexia? *British Journal of Special Education, 38*(4), 191–200.

Nugent, M. (2007). Comparing inclusive and segregated settings for children with dyslexia—Parental perspectives from Ireland. *Support for Learning, 22*(2), 52–59.

Shaywitz, S. E., & Shaywitz, J. (2020). *Overcoming dyslexia: Completely revised and updated*. Hachette UK.

11

Motivating Children with Dyslexia to Read

Motivating Children with Dyslexia to Read Explained

We enjoy participating in our preferred activities and we often avoid activities in which we struggle. For our children with dyslexia, reading is a struggle. As a parent, you have experiences with your child practicing reading at home. You recognize the struggle is real and at times reading is a frustrating experience for you and your child. That's no surprise when you consider your child may have already been at school for six hours that day with both traditional and special education reading instruction, then must come home and spend time completing homework. Add in tutoring and additional reading practice and no wonder your child feels overwhelmed. It can also be frustrating for you when your child is not motivated to read. This impedes completing homework and largely eliminates reading as one of your child's leisure time activities. Therefore, we believe it's important to find some alternative ways to reinforce reading and writing to help motivate your child.

This chapter addresses different ways you can work with your child to reinforce literacy skills in a more enjoyable manner. Since reading is hard work and can be frustrating, it's important

DOI: 10.4324/9781003400615-12

to remember that some reading time is better than none. If your child has a low frustration tolerance, *sometimes it is better to stop then to push on with the activity. This benefits your relationship with your child.* Try again another day.

What the Research Reports

It is challenging to motivate children with dyslexia to read. Melekoglu and Wilkerson (2013) studied motivation in children with and without dyslexia and reported, "No significant change in motivation to read of students with disabilities from pretest to posttest; all their motivation scores declined" (p. 85). On the contrary, their research found the motivation scores of adolescents without disabilities increased.

Researchers (Bender & Wall, 1994; Chapman et al., 2000; Morgan et al., 2008) have acknowledged that when children are not motivated to read it creates a negative cycle which can place your child at a long-term disadvantage. In simple terms, here is what happens when your child with dyslexia avoids reading. Children with a negative attitude toward reading:

- ◆ Avoid reading for pleasure
- ◆ Develop a limited bank of vocabulary words
- ◆ Miss the development of critical reading skills and strategies
- ◆ Lack reading comprehension
- ◆ Find reading a less enjoyable pastime
- ◆ Avoid reading school textbooks

Therefore, a lack of reading motivation impedes skill development of strategies needed for academic success. Struggling readers often cannot derive meaning from what they read, and thus, their motivation to read decreases. As noted by Soriano-Ferrer & Morte-Soriano (2017), this is the Matthew effect of accumulated advantage where "the rich get richer and the poor get poorer" but in this case it's the better readers become best and the worst readers stay worst. Unfortunately, many children with dyslexia don't read and therefore remain poor readers.

Research has shown that increasing time that students read independently as well as giving students a choice of text are two factors that can increase a students' enjoyment of reading and reading motivation (Allred & Cena, 2020). Furthermore, Gooch and colleagues (2016) found that children have increased when reading is game-like. They call this concept "gamification" or the use of game elements, such as digital rewards, in non-game contexts. The authors concluded, "The results of our study show that gamification can foster student motivation, in this instance due to an interaction between a highly customisable design and pedagogically tailored appropriation by teachers" (p. 10).

While it is challenging to motivate children with dyslexia to read, it's not impossible. To motivate your child to read, it takes intentionality and creativity on your part as well as incorporating technology, and your child's interests. Specialized instruction and motivational activities can change your child's attitude toward reading. Together you can make reading enjoyable.

Quick Start to Motivating Children with Dyslexia to Read

As a parent, at home you can reinforce the skills and strategies your child is learning in school. The more your child is exposed to text, and perhaps listens to text that is within their understanding level but above their independent reading level, the better. Let's explore some ways that may be motivating and support the reading process for your child.

Technology Tips

There are many types of technology that are at our fingertips every day. There is a plethora of apps that work on reading skills across phonemic awareness, phonics, fluency, vocabulary and comprehension. Before choosing an app or computer game, consider the apps purpose. Many are game based, but there should be a clear educational component to it. Table 11.1 has some

TABLE 11.1 Technology Apps for Reading

Reading Area	Technology app	Description	Resource
Phonemic awareness	Phonemic Awareness Bubbles	This app focuses on sound discrimination	Available on iOS
Phonics	Homer Learn & Grow	Fun early learning app for reading. Children can read stories, draw, play games that all develop their reading skills	Available on iOS and Android
Fluency	Reading Eggs	Develops fluency via games and interactive activities. Parents can also monitor their student's progress	Available on iOS and Android
Vocabulary	Endless Alphabet	Develops vocabulary through interactive games that teach phonics and letter identification as well as definitions of words	Available on iOS and Android
Comprehension	Epic!	Offers a large library of interactive books which can be read aloud to the student	www.getepic.com/available on iOS, Android
Comprehension Writing	Voki	Use Voki to make an Avatar which can be used to tell a story or answer comprehension questions	www.voki.com

suggested apps across the reading areas. Try it yourself to see how appropriate it may be for your child.

Fun Ways to Incorporate Writing

Writing has been shown to have positive effects on reading ability. There are many motivating ways to increase your child's desire to write without using the typical pencil and paper way. Consider these:

♦ If your child enjoys reading graphic novels, how interested would they be in writing their own? There are applications that do this such as *Comic Life*. For the "no tech" option, you can certainly have your child create a comic strip with paper and pencil. David Wayne Chiu provides a guide you can use. *Create Your Own Graphic Novel: A Guide for Kids: Write and Draw Your Own Book* on Amazon.

♦ Assist your child in writing their own book. You can use paper or purchase a "blank book" (see resources). For example, write an "All About Me" book. Cut or print out pictures using your child's favorite foods, color, toys, interests, or family members. Secure them to the blank page and assist your child in writing one or more sentences about the picture. This becomes a motivating book for your child to read with you and others.

♦ Going to the grocery store? Need to make a list? Have your child assist you with making a list for shopping or your to-do list for the week.

♦ Try using an app such as *ChatterPix*, that will bring any object to "life" and can speak. Your child can create a simple story using this app and can have the object tell its story.

♦ Many kids enjoy doing mazes and you can suggest that your child create his or her own mazes for others to complete. You can use graph paper to help with the lines or just use blank paper. Your child can write the directions so people know what to do because some mazes are started at the end, are completed with the opposite hand, or get penalized if they hit a dead-end.

♦ Give your child a life skill that is crucial in today's world. Use Type to Learn, Mavis Beacon, or another keyboarding program and require 10-15 minutes of daily keyboard training. Proficiency in typing can make your child's life easier.

Audio Books

Most children with dyslexia enjoy being read to. There are ample opportunities for technology to read to your child.

♦ Use audiobooks to expose your child to text that may be above their reading grade level but not their understanding grade level. This can be done while you are in the car to or from school or perhaps on a personal device such as an iPad

♦ Use Audible to have a home device read an audiobook

♦ Subscribe to Learning Ally to access their catalog of books on audio

Reading Using Song Lyrics

Do you use music to help motivate you to exercise or complete a task? You can use music song lyrics to help motivate your child to read. Search the internet for your child's favorite song lyrics and then print them out. You can use the lyrics to enhance several areas of reading. We'll use the Jack and Jill nursery rhyme as an example.

Jack and Jill went up a hill to fetch a pail of water. Jack fell down and broke his crown and Jill came tumbling after.

You can reinforce these reading areas with your child:

♦ Phonics: Circle all the words that start with the /j/ sound; underline the words that end with the "ill" word family

♦ Fluency: Read the rhyme together the first emphasizing fluency and second emphasizing expression

♦ Vocabulary: Discuss the meaning of crown, fetch, tumbling

◆ Comprehension: Ask questions such as, "Why did they go up the hill? What do you think caused Jack to fall?"

Apply this same process if your child enjoys reading poetry.

Find a Reading Series They Love

Children are motivated to read when they have a favorite series. Peggy explained, "My son loved the *Left Behind: The Kids* series so much it was like binge reading instead of Netflix video binging. *Left Behind: The Kids* has 40 books so he was engaged for months." Locate a series for your child by searching Amazon using the key words "reading series."

Graphic Novels

The Baby-Sitters Club, Spy School, Dog Man, and *Percy Jackson* are popular graphic novels for young kids. Children with dyslexia gravitate toward graphic novels because these books are less overwhelming. Graphic novels have more colorful pictures and fewer words. Encourage your child's graphic novel reading as these are stepping stones toward reading more advanced content.

Reading Magazines

Yes, magazines still exist! There are colorful magazines for kids such as Sports Illustrated for Kids, Zoobooks, Time for Kids, chickaDEE, Highlights, and Nickelodeon Magazine. Many are available in your school or local library. Use the same process described above for reinforcing reading using song lyrics with magazine articles.

Use Interests

One author understands reading struggles because he had a hard time reading and sounding out words. However, he had a strong memory and compensated by memorizing. During his childhood it was common to collect things so as a ten-year-old kid he collected beer cans. His dad drank the beer and James used shelving to display each can's colorful design. His parents subscribed him to Beer Can Collectors of America and he read articles about beer cans. They took him on the brewery tour at

Busch Gardens. While these did not lead to his career, the activities motivated him to read.

If your child has an interest in Minecraft, use this to help learn sight words. Make flashcards using a Minecraft type font. You could create a fun way to memorize sight words by making a Minecraft flashcard concentration game. Or, you and your child can staple paper together and use some sight words to write a story about your son and Minecraft. He can practice reading the story which can motivate him to read.

You might locate material for your child to read about his or her interests in Pokémon, space, sports, arts and crafts, or Candy Crush. Support your child's reading interests with content and fun experiences.

Pay Them to Read

Money motivates some children. James was listening to a best-selling author and leadership expert, speak about his childhood experiences. This expert explained that rather than getting paid an allowance to do childhood chores like take out the garbage, his parents paid him to read a book and write a one-page summary. The purpose of this was not to devalue the benefits of chores but rather that parents could invest money into nurturing their child's literacy skills. If reading print is too hard for your child then allow them to listen to an audiobook and then write up the report.

Set Goals

Most children read less than 15 minutes per day. The amount of time that children read directly impacts their achievement. Set goals for your child to read and keep track of those goals. It is motivating for students to set reading goals, monitor them, and reach those goals. Think of incentives for your child as they meet their time spent reading goals. Use a graph to track their goals or an app such as *Bookroo*, to help monitor and track your child's reading progress.

Summary

Making reading fun helps increase your child's motivation for reading. Finding ways to integrate reading at home using different strategies and technology tools are some ways to increase the amount of time your child will spend reading. As the Matthew effect says, the more a child reads and is exposed to text, the more likely their reading achievement will increase. Specialized instruction combined with motivational activities can change your child's attitude toward reading.

Resources

Blank Books: www.barebooks.com
Bookroo Reading tracker, set custom goals for your child: https://bookroo.com/parents
Chatterpix, Make anything talk and come to life: https://apps.apple.com/us/app/chatterpix-kids/id734046126
Comic Life, Make comic strips digitally: http://comiclife.com/
Kids Listen, 6 Minute Podcast: https://app.kidslisten.org/ep/Six-Minutes-S1-E1-Six-Minutes-Begins

Chapter References

Allred, J. B., & Cena, M. E. (2020). Reading motivation in high school: Instructional shifts in student choice and class time. *Journal of Adolescent & Adult Literacy, 64*(1), 27–35.

Bender, W. B., & Wall, M. E. (1994). Social-emotional development of students with learning disabilities. *Learning Disability Quarterly, 17*, 323–341.

Chapman, J. W., Tunmer, W. E., & Prochnow, J. E. (2000). Early reading-related skills and performance, reading self-concept, and the development of academic self-concept: A longitudinal study. *Journal of Educational Psychology, 92*, 703–708.

Gooch, D., Vasalou, A., Benton, L., & Khaled, R. (2016, May). Using gamification to motivate students with dyslexia. In *Proceedings of the 2016 CHI Conference on human factors in computing systems* (pp. 969–980).

Melekoglu, M. A., & Wilkerson, K. L. (2013). Motivation to read: How does it change for struggling readers with and without disabilities? *International Journal of Instruction, 6*(1), 77–88.

Morgan, P. L., Fuchs, D., Compton, D. L., Cordray, D. S., & Fuchs, L. S. (2008). Does early reading failure decrease children's reading motivation? *Journal of Learning Disabilities, 41*(5), 387–404.

Soriano-Ferrer, M., & Morte-Soriano, M. (2017). Teacher perceptions of reading motivation in children with developmental dyslexia and average readers. *Procedia-Social and Behavioral Sciences, 237*, 50–56.

12

Nurturing Talent and Creativity in Your Child with Dyslexia

Creativity Explained

Reflect on what you excel at or feel smart about. What is it? You probably thought of one or more areas where you have talent or smarts. We all need to feel and believe that we are good at something because this helps us develop our self-esteem. Healthy self-esteem is necessary for success in life. Self-esteem is developed by combining our internal beliefs with our external feedback. Thus, self-esteem is a combination of how we view ourselves and how we believe others view us.

We want your child with dyslexia to develop healthy self-esteem and feel good about him or herself. What area(s) does your child believe they are good? Although it might be academic related, it does not have to be. Perhaps your child believes she is talented at mathematics. Others might believe they are science experts with a deep knowledge of space, fossils, or rocks. Your child's natural talent might be athletics and being one of the fastest runners, best basketball free throwers, dancer, or figure skater. Does your child have innate musical ability with singing or playing instruments? Whatever your

DOI: 10.4324/9781003400615-13

child's strength area is, acknowledge it and verbally reinforce it in a genuine way.

In other words, your child knows when you are giving 'lip service' or when your words are heartfelt. We give our kids two types of praise: general or specific, and there is a time to use both. You give specific praise when you tell your son he put a mighty swing into hitting the ball or when you tell your daughter her form on the springboard was outstanding. Even if your child is not a stellar student, they appreciate it when you comment on their effort. If your son despises going to school, he might appreciate it when you comment, "You got yourself up and out of bed on time today. Thanks, and that helped the morning go much more smoothly." We give general praise by saying, "Nice job," "Way to go," or "Great work on your project."

Your praise, encouragement, and support in your child's early years matters. We've worked with many parents of children with dyslexia and many shared their true and time-tested advice which we'll share with you. Christina offers this advice:

> I would say to never forget that your child is always look- ing to you for support and motivation. The way you react to your child's special need can really pave the way for how they feel about themselves. I always try to remain positive, but also realistic with Eli. I tell him to take his time and explain to him that some things may be a bit more difficult for him to learn at first, but he should never give up.

Gretchen explains:

> The most important thing was getting her the appropri- ate tutoring with the Orton Gillingham instruction. It was extra time and money, but worth it in the long run. The other important thing was helping our daughter build self-confidence by helping her understand that dyslexia has nothing to do with her intelligence but just that her

brain learns and processes differently than other people. And that it can be a gift!

Tracy explained:

> Instill a passion for reading. She was read to nightly and starting early we read novels to while she would follow along (like the Harry Potter series). This got her interested in books and the powerful stories hidden below the covers. Her desire to read helped her immensely

Linda put it this way:

> I taught him that his dyslexia is his super power and because his brain works differently, he had a different, unique viewpoint from the other "usual" thinking people like me!

Kaylie believes:

> Give continued encouragement and reinforcement. For a child that struggles and knows it, giving her confidence is key. She achieved that through sports and continued reinforcement in academic activities she is good at.

These parents offered heartfelt information to encourage you that your child has strengths and that reading can improve. Your child can become self-sufficient. And, your child can develop good self-esteem.

What the Research Reports

Is dyslexia a type of superpower that automatically makes dyslexics more creative than non-dyslexics? In short, "No." Certainly when you search the internet for famous dyslexics many recognizable names appear including Tim Tebow, Barbara Corcoran, Daymond John, Jennifer Aniston, Whoopi Goldberg, Danny

Glover, Tom Cruise, Charles Schwab, and many more. Yet for every famous person with dyslexia, there are just as many people with dyslexia who are average folk. In the 2020 book, *Overcoming Dyslexia*, Shaywitz and Shaywitz write they often compare dyslexia to an iceberg that is 90% hidden underwater. Society sees the successful individuals at the top but we must not forget the 90% of dyslexics who are underwater and unseen.

Consider any field such as medicine, athletics, law, business, finance, etc., and there is always a small percentage of people that reach the elite or extremely successful level. So, it is not surprising that a percentage of people with dyslexia also reach the pinnacle of success. We write this not to discourage you but rather to encourage you to continually call out your child's natural talents and strengths. Highly successful people with dyslexia show there is no ceiling for people with dyslexia.

But, by no means are we Pollyannas, as we recognize children with dyslexia struggle and may have severe struggles. Our point is that you should never write your child off by thinking, "They are not a good reader now so they will probably never become a good reader." Children with dyslexia continue to develop and today's struggles could become future strengths. Your child has resilience. He may be down, but not out. She might be discouraged but not defeated. His perceived laziness can grow into a love. Your child is in a temporary season and with your support, advocacy, and encouragement and their hard work, circumstances change. Keep pushing through and nurturing your child's natural affinities.

Many people believe dyslexics are more creative than non-dyslexics. In their meta-analysis, Majeed and colleagues (2021) offer two explanations for this.

First, the compensation hypothesis posits that individuals with dyslexia undergo compensatory neurological development in other brain structures to counteract deficits caused by dyslexia, such as the left anterior inferior frontal gyrus and the lateral frontopolar cortex, both of which have been associated with creativity.

(p. 2)

Second,

> The early choice hypothesis, on the other hand, suggests that higher levels of creativity among individuals with dyslexia arise due to practice effects that stem from adopting non-typical methods early on, such as using pictures rather than words, to process information.
>
> (p. 2)

The results of their meta-analysis were: "Overall, the meta-analytic results showed that there was no significant difference between groups with and without developmental dyslexia in their creativity scores" (p. 10). The authors explained that these differences did not appear in children with dyslexia but were in fact noted in adults with dyslexia.

Researchers Erbeli and colleagues (2022) completed a meta-analysis and their findings supported those of Majeed and colleagues. Their study found that, as a group, individuals with dyslexia were no more creative than peers without dyslexia.

If dyslexics are not more creative, then don't they at least have better visual spatial thinking? Von Karolyi and colleagues (2003) found people with dyslexia were better at seeing the big picture with their visual spatial abilities than the individual pieces.

However, this was not always the case as documented by Giovagnoli and colleagues (2016). In their meta-analysis they found children with developmental dyslexia had deficits in several visual-spatial abilities that might actually contribute to lower reading skills. This was supported by Chamberlain and colleagues who concluded, "This meta-analysis demonstrates that participants with dyslexia perform less well on tests of visuospatial ability" (p. 908).

While researchers have not completely confirmed abundant talents in dyslexics as a whole, many dyslexia experts support "hidden talents" or "seas of strength" in those with dyslexia. Drs. Brock and Bernette Eide take a strength-based approach to dyslexia and in their book, *The Dyslexia Advantage: Unlocking the Hidden Potential of the Dyslexic Brain,* they acknowledge that many people with dyslexia have hardships but offer the MIND approach to growth. Individuals with dyslexia typically have strength in one or more areas of Material, Interconnected, Narrative, or Dynamic Reasoning. With this approach people with dyslexia can become successful if they persist, use proven approaches, technology, give continual effort, become self-advocates, and make use of their strengths to give themselves the dyslexia advantage.

Ben Foss wrote *The Dyslexia Empowerment Plan: A Blueprint for Renewing Your Child's Confidence and Love of Learning*. He describes his own struggles with dyslexia and provides parents with a new perspective that remediating what is broken in your child is not the ultimate goal. He explains, "There are specific attitudes and habits that will have a huge impact on whether your child will be able to apply her strengths at school and beyond" (pp. 80–81). Foss provided an Attitudes Star assessment you can take to help you recognize and build upon your child's strengths. Dyslexia does not equate to disaster but rather it equates to the need for hard work, specialized instruction, and parental support.

Quick Start Guide to Nurturing Talent and Creativity

There are different ways to conceptualize intelligence and professor Dr. Howard Gardner explained this using a multiple intelligences explanation. In 1983 he wrote, *Frames of Mind: The Theory of Multiple Intelligences* which explained people can have intelligence in: visual-spatial, bodily-kinesthetic, linguistic, interpersonal, logical, musical, and interpersonal abilities. He later added another intelligence called naturistic. Dr. Gardner's theory helps us understand children can be smart in different ways and children with dyslexia are no exception. Below is a summary of each intelligence and possible activities you might use to build your child's multiple intelligences.

Visual-Spatial Intelligence
These children can mentally visualize the spatial world in their mind's eye. They think in pictures and images so they visualize how things fit together, whether mechanical or artistic.

Individuals with strong visual-spatial abilities might have careers as an engineer, surveyor, architect, urban planner, fashion designer, graphic artist, interior decorator, photographer, or pilot.

To nurture visual-spatial strengths you might have your child:

TABLE 12.1 Nurturing Visual-Spatial Strengths

Create and edit videos	Play Roblox	Build Lego sets
Play the Tetris video game	Visit a corn maze	Create your own mazes
Color	Create a mural	Build with Lincoln Logs
Use Perler beads to create designs	Volunteer to take pictures	Visit art galleries
Draw with Crayola Light Up tracing pad coloring board	Build with Picasso tiles	Play Minecraft

Bodily-Kinesthetic Intelligence

These children are physical and enjoy using their body to convey feelings or ideas or they may skillfully handle tools, utensils, or sports equipment. They think in movements and use their body, in part or whole, to create, learn, process, and problem solve. These individuals may enjoy jobs such as physical therapist, contractor, fire fighter, dancer, actor, mechanic, carpenter, athlete, or jeweler.

Consider these activities if you want to develop or enhance your child's bodily-kinesthetic intelligence:

TABLE 12.2 Nurturing Bodily-Kinesthetic Intelligence

Build your own computer	Play games like Cornhole	Learn how to juggle
Take gymnastics lessons	Play the game Twister	Learn how to weave or sew
Bike ride	Create a friendship bracelet	Create scavenger hunts
Learn to rock climb	Visit trampoline parks	Construct a model car, boat, or plane
Jump rope	Take drama or acting lessons	Play sports

Linguistic Intelligence

These children enjoy words. Reading, writing, and vocabulary are all areas where these children excel. Many enjoy learning languages. They can explain information to others. Individuals with Linguistic strength may excel in careers as a writer, editor, politician, preacher, actor, speech pathologist, salesperson, entrepreneur, writer, radio or TV announcer, advertising executive, or journalist.

Consider these activities if you want to develop or enhance your child's linguistic intelligence:

TABLE 12.3 Nurturing Linguistic Intelligence

Take debate lessons or join a debate club	Learn a foreign language	Create a podcast
Write poems	Play words with friends	Create your own newsletter
Volunteer to read books to younger children	Play games like Boggle Jr. or Scrabble Flash	Start a blog
Listen to stories or age-appropriate TED talks	Write and self-publish a book	Interview others
Self-publish your own greeting cards	Learn sign language and volunteer to sign	Learn one new vocabulary word per day or week

Interpersonal Intelligence

These children are people smart, sociable, compassionate and enjoy being with others. They are naturally skilled at working with groups or on teams. They have the gift of mediation, communication, and negotiation. People with these strengths might have careers including administrator, manager, personnel worker, psychologist, nurse, public relations person, social director, or teacher.

Consider these activities if you want to develop or enhance your child's Interpersonal intelligence:

TABLE 12.4 Nurturing Interpersonal Intelligence

Create entertaining videos to show others	Volunteer as a helper in Sunday school or similar	Volunteer or try out for performances
Perform puppet shows	Set up a lemonade stand	Play games such as Sims or Club Penguin
Volunteer to help a teacher	Tutor younger students	Volunteer at pet shelter
Play board games such as Life® Monopoly ® or Sorry ®	Visit nursing homes	Join a church group or religious group for kids
Run for student government	Volunteer at the Special Olympics or a Special Needs Walk	Join team sports

Logical-Mathematical Intelligence

These children are strong with logic and are powerful thinkers. They can reason, think in numbers, identify patterns, and enjoy making connections among different sources of information. They are critical thinkers asking thoughtful questions. Individuals with these strengths may have a career as a doctor, attorney, researcher, auditor, accountant, bookkeeper, electrician, project manager, detective, logistics manager, mathematician, financial planner, scientist, statistician, computer analyst, or technician.

Consider these activities if you want to develop or enhance your child's logical-mathematical intelligence:

TABLE 12.5 Nurturing Logical-Mathematical Intelligence

Learn to play chess	Learn about the stock market or investing	Play Exploding Kittens Card Game (ages 7+)
Play the Hasbro Game Guess Who? Classic	Play Blokus strategy board game	Play the board game Dragonwood: A Game of Dice & Daring
Join a math club	Learn to code using Move The Turtle or Kodable	Play Rummikub
Create your own code language of new written symbols	Create computer codes using Tynker	Watch Kahn Academy Math Videos
Use *The Everything Kids Science Experiments Book*	Use a scale to weigh & compare different objects	Use the 4M Crystal Growing Experiment

Musical Intelligence

These children have a natural ability to understand and use music, sounds, instruments, and voice. They think in sounds, rhythms, melodies, and rhymes. Musically talented people might have careers including musician, piano tuner, music therapist, choral director, conductor, music producer, or worship leader.

Consider these activities if you want to develop or enhance your child's musical intelligence:

TABLE 12.6 Nurturing Musical Intelligence

Start a band	Volunteer with a local theatre production	Watch Broadway musicals on streaming networks
Volunteer to teach an instrument to a younger child	Use music and math to practice times tables with Math Rockx	Create videos of yourself singing and show them to family or friends
Create original mixes and share with others	Listen to music from different historical periods	Play music games e.g., The Voice
Watch music shows such as Glee or American Idol	Learn to play a new instrument	Re-write lyrics of your favorite songs
Mix music with DJ app	Write songs, compose music	Learn the program Garage Band

Intrapersonal Intelligence

These children are self-aware or introspective. They understand who they are and don't necessarily mind alone time. They understand their needs and can internally process how their decisions have consequences. These children may not always prefer to work alone but they are keenly aware of their learning preference. They may have careers as a psychologist, therapist, counselor, theologian, writer, program planner, or entrepreneur.

Consider these activities if you want to develop or enhance your child's intrapersonal intelligence:

TABLE 12.7 Nurturing Intrapersonal Intelligence

Build using clay or play dough	Research family genealogy	Write out your goals
Visit museums	Color	Create a scrapbook
Do yoga	Read or watch biographies	Start to collect things
Start a blog	Solve jigsaw puzzles	Play Kahoot
Solve brain teasers or riddles	Keep a diary	Make photo albums, books, slide shows

Naturalistic Intelligence

These children love nature and being outdoors. They often have a heightened ability to notice details about animals, weather, Earth, water, trees, and plants. They relate to animals, enjoy gardening, and digging. They think by observing, recognizing, and classifying items in the natural environment. Adults with naturalistic strength may have careers as a botanist, astronomer, wildlife illustrator, meteorologist, farmer, zoo curator, park ranger, geologist, or landscaper.

Consider these activities if you want to develop or enhance your child's naturalistic intelligence:

TABLE 12.8 Nurturing Naturalistic Intelligence

Collect natural organisms or rocks	Make a bird feeder and bird watch	Become a junior ranger at state or national parks
Explore using Google Earth	Go kayaking, canoeing, stand up paddle boarding	Care for pets or plants
Research animal habitats	Go geocaching	Start an outdoor business
Build a treehouse or fort	Plant a tree	Volunteer on Earth Day
Go fishing	Go camping or hiking	Create a terrarium with Creativity for Kids Grow N Glow Kit

Summary

Creativity, talent, smarts, and natural affinities are words to describe your child's gifts and abilities. Since children develop at different rates you can provide your child with opportunities to sample various activities, athletics, arts, and hobbies to gauge their interest and talents in these. Some activities will be tried and shelved while others might continue to develop and refine through adolescence and into adulthood. It's often our natural strengths that carry us through in life and shape our career choices. Your child is smart in many ways so help other family members and teachers understand your child's natural assets.

Resources

The National Society of Creative Dyslexics has resources to empower dyslexia through remediation and understanding: http://creativedyslexics.org

The website for the Drs Eide who wrote the book *The Dyslexia Advantage: Unlocking the Hidden Potential of the Dyslexic Brain*: www.dyslexicadvantage.org

The Yale Center for Dyslexia and Creativity has resources and information about advocating and helping people with dyslexia reach their full potential: www.dyslexia.yale.edu

The Dyslexia Initiative was created to support families, and their dyslexic children: www.thedyslexiainitiative.org

Chapter References

Chamberlain, R., Brunswick, N., Siev, J., & McManus, I. C. (2018). Meta-analytic findings reveal lower means but higher variances in visuospatial ability in dyslexia. *British Journal of Psychology, 109*(4), 897–916.

Eide, B. L., & Eide, F. F. (2012). *The dyslexic advantage: Unlocking the hidden potential of the dyslexic brain*. Penguin.

Erbeli, F., Peng, P., & Rice, M. (2022). No evidence of creative benefit accompanying dyslexia: A meta-analysis. *Journal of Learning Disabilities*, *55*(3), 242–253.

Foss, B. (2013). *The dyslexia empowerment plan: A blueprint for renewing your child's confidence and love of learning.* Ballantine Books.

Gardner, H. (1983). *Frames of mind. The theory of multiple intelligence.* Basic Books.

Giovagnoli, G., Vicari, S., Tomassetti, S., & Menghini, D. (2016). The role of visual-spatial abilities in dyslexia: Age differences in children's reading? *Frontiers in Psychology*, *7*, 1997.

Majeed, N. M., Hartanto, A., & Tan, J. J. (2021). Developmental dyslexia and creativity: A meta-analysis. *Dyslexia*, *27*(2), 187–203.

Shaywitz, S. E., & Shaywitz, J. (2020). *Overcoming dyslexia: Completely revised and updated.* Hachette UK.

Von Karolyi, C., Winner, E., Gray, W., & Sherman, G. F. (2003). Dyslexia linked to talent: Global visual-spatial ability. *Brain and Language*, *85*(3), 427–431.

Printed in the United States
by Baker & Taylor Publisher Services